Mw...

Astrology and the Royal Family

Astrology and the Royal Family

Roger Elliot

Pan Books London and Sydney

Published 1977 by Pan Books Ltd,
Cavaye Place, London SW10 9PG
© Roger Elliot 1977
ISBN 0 330 24710 7
Printed and bound in England by
Hazell Watson & Viney Ltd, Aylesbury, Bucks

Contents

Introduction

The King and Queen paid me a visit when I was five years old. At least, they drove past the school gates, and the whole kindergarten class, along with the rest of sleepy Torquay, crowded the pavements, waved Union flags and raised a genteel hullabaloo as the royal limousine passed.

I think I saw them. But perhaps I fidgeted at the last minute and missed my moment of history. Perhaps, anyway, it was not the Royal Family at all, but those other war heroes, Winnie and Clemmie Churchill. To my childish mind there was no distinction between Head of State and Head of Government. All of them were leading us in the fight against Germany, a faraway country I took to be Berry Head, eight miles across Tor Bay.

I knew the King best of all, for his sidelong head appeared on the pennies I was given to buy Mars Bars. If it wasn't his own youngish, vulnerable, adam's-appled profile on the coin, it would be his father's, the old King, moustachioed and a bit gruff, or the bald, pompous countenance of his grandfather. Postage stamps, too, were my portrait gallery of this famous family. Sometimes, torn and fading, the stamps of the great-grandmother of them all, Queen Victoria, would come into my possession. She, it appeared, had invented the British Empire which ran across the face of the world, like spilt red ink, from Australia to the West Indies. Much fresher, but rarely seen, were the schoolboy features of Edward VIII. There was a mystery here. He seemed younger and more likeable than all the others, and he was not a parent, merely a brother, of the present king. He was not dead. Something naughty had happened. He had disappeared.

Gradually, as I grew up, I encountered the rest of the family – the two Princesses Elizabeth and Margaret Rose, haughty Queen Mary, and numerous lesser Royals. Their images were

7

everywhere – the newspapers, *Picture Post*, Gaumont-British News, biscuit boxes and commemoration mugs and the Crawfie books that my mother brought home from the public library. They were, at once, familiar and utterly remote. They kept on performing a succession of astounding duties – going to sunny South Africa in the middle of winter in a battleship, going to the cinema in glittering evening frocks, waving from fairy-tale coaches and getting married on the day we had a school holiday.

Suddenly one day, when I came out of chemistry class, the flag was at half-mast. 'King's dead,' I was told. It all seemed a bit excessive. King was a boy in the lower fifth, a nonentity really. When the truth dawned that *the* King had died, an ineffable *frisson* swept through my being. I knew, with the mounting inner excitement of a teenage Cancerian, that this was a Momentous Calamity, and I would love every minute of it: the solemn music on the radio, the purple edging on the school copy of the *Daily Graphic*, the guns and muffled drums and the sight of the banished Duke of Windsor, suddenly a middle-aged man, allowed home for this special occasion.

Next came the new Elizabethan Age. None of us really believed in it. Already there was too wide a credibility gap between the kings and queens of fancy-dress history, with their battles and round-the-world expeditions and grand swanky ways, and our mild, polite, modern Royal Family who opened hospitals, had nannies for their children, spoke pure, clear English and wouldn't offend a fly.

As my generation became adult, we learnt to criticize the Royals. They were a lot of middle-class, philistine squares with too much money and too little knowledge of the real world. How dare the Queen still send her children to public schools! Why the hell shouldn't Princess Margaret marry Group-Captain Townsend? Oughtn't they all to ride bicycles, get ordinary jobs, mix freely with you, me and the postman? And what about the poor old Duke of Windsor? Don't they *care*?

But this cynicism was always tinged with respect. The public attitude towards royalty was as schizophrenic as the royal way of life itself. One side of the Royal Family's lifestyle was public, blameless and totally visible. But their private lives, once the

8

carriages had swept back to Buckingham Palace, were unknown and deliberately kept secret. Mystique surrounded their official rituals, and mystery shrouded their personal heartbreaks and joys and scandals. They resembled old-style prima donnas – immaculate, fabulous creatures on stage but unimaginable as ordinary mortals. No wonder we were avid for gossip, relishing the footman's memoirs and the anecdotes of the friend of a friend who went to one of Tony and Margaret's parties!

It was about the same time – the later 1960s – that I became fascinated by astrology, and the Royal Family obsessed by publicity. Just as I was discovering a unique means of understanding the human personality, the Royal Family, helped by public relations experts, were beginning to show that they were human after all and had individual personalities. Charles and Anne were launched into public life and these two young people were obviously more relaxed and humorous and opinionated than earlier royal generations. The whole family, in fact, appeared in their own 110-minute television film as relaxed, humorous and sometimes opinionated individuals. Monarchy in Britain, in short, was given a facelift. The Queen apart, members of the family gave interviews and appeared on television programmes. The Queen herself made 'walkabouts', mixing with ordinary people. When inflation hit the world in the 1970s, the Royal Family was hit as hard as anybody: Philip sold his yacht and the Queen cancelled a quarter-million-pound redecoration of her country house, Sandringham.

But the facelift changed nothing except the external image of royalty in the eyes of the world. The central mysteries remained: who were these people in reality? What were their strengths and weaknesses, their talents, their passions and hatreds? How would they have fared in the hurly-burly of ordinary life without benefit of wealth, privilege and special training? Were they, as many people believed, genuinely extraordinary, a family apart, with almost a divine aura due to their royal position?

These are questions which no amount of public exposure can ever answer, for simply observing people's behaviour, however honest and straightforward it may be, never reveals the true wellsprings of human character. Nor can in-depth interviews necessarily help, even if we can imagine Her Majesty submitting to such a probing analysis, for people's ideas about themselves can be as false as the wildest gossip.

I became convinced that astrology could be the key to unlock these mysteries. I knew that the horoscope – a map of the solar system at the moment of birth – was an uncanny guide to that person's true inner temperament. By studying the birth-charts of each member of the Royal Family, starting with the founder of modern royalty, Queen Victoria, I should have an unrivalled view of their real characters. Much of it, naturally, would tally with known facts. But some surprising new insights could emerge.

What's more, astrology is a method of prediction as much as character analysis. I could look ahead to see what lies in store for the Queen and her family – to see their constitutional future as well as their individual destinies, for the fate of Britain and the Commonwealth as a monarchy is intimately bound up with the fate of the Royal Family as a whole.

I could even look back in the past and 'predict' what happened when Victoria met Albert, or Edward VII espied Lily Langtry, or, best of all, what drew the Prince of Wales and Mrs Simpson together. I might throw light on unresolved mysteries such as the relationship between Queen Victoria and her servant, John Brown. And I could guess at the course of English royal life had Prince Albert Victor, the dissolute eldest son of Edward VII, ever ascended the Throne.

This book is the fruit of my studies. You will learn something about astrology itself and a good deal about the Royal Family. But before we begin our exploration of the royal stars, I must deal with an ethical problem which may seem unreal, in view of the countless books about the Royal Family already written, but which matters to me.

I believe that the moment of birth is one's second private possession, in the same way that one's body is one's first possession. In effect, your body and horoscope are born together, and each of them is a diagram of your identity – the body by means of the unique DNA code within its cellular structure, and the horoscope through its unique pattern of planets. Just as the law of *habeas corpus* lays down that each of us, so to speak, owns our own body, so should there be a similar recognition that our horoscope belongs to us and should not be stolen by any Tom, Dick or Harry.

In this book I am stealing the contents of Her Majesty's horoscope without any gracious permission at all, as well as those of her relatives. To them all I offer a sincere apology. It cannot be much fun to be stared at, pulled to pieces, satirized and exposed as comprehensively as they must endure, without much chance to answer back. We, after all, can fidget, lose our flag, go to sleep or walk away from the hubbub altogether. They are trapped in the royal limousine for eternity.

How astrology works

Many people's knowledge of astrology is limited to their 'Lucky Stars' columns in newspapers and magazines. They read their daily quota of good news or bad luck, under the twelve Zodiac signs, and believe that's the end of the matter.

Not at all. Real astrology is a complex science that takes years to master. It involves an array of mystical-sounding jargon, such as planets, houses, signs, aspects and transits, plus a good deal of mathematical expertise, before the art of astrological interpretation can begin. To enjoy your stroll through the royal portrait gallery, you must understand the basic astrological techniques.

Astrology is the study of the heavens to see what impact, if any, they have on events on Earth. The theory is simple: it asserts that a person's character can be known from birth. At the moment that an infant takes its first breath, the heavenly bodies surrounding the Earth form a particular pattern (a few minutes earlier it would have been a slightly different pattern; a few minutes later, different again). This pattern, or map of the sky, is known as the horoscope, and it forms the key to understanding that particular child's personality.

It is not a map of the whole starry galaxy. The stars, indeed, are left out altogether. The important factors are the Sun, Moon and planets which form the solar system surrounding Earth. These are our nearest neighbours in space – our heavenly 'family', in effect. And just as a child is moulded by the influence of parents and other relatives, so, according to astrology, is it affected by its heavenly parents, the Sun and Moon, and its heavenly siblings, Mercury, Venus, Mars and so on.

Each planet in the solar system represents a particular element in our psychological make-up. It also has its own symbol:

☉ **Sun** Our inner character. The part of us that needs to be expressed in the outside world through work, creative activities and social contacts. What we want to *do* in life.

☽ **Moon** Our emotional disposition. The way we react to circumstances around us. This is often a private part of our personalities that only close friends – and ourselves, of course – will recognize. How we *feel* about life.

☿ **Mercury** Our mental faculties. Our way of perceiving the world, putting together ideas, expressing ourselves in words and arguments. How we *think* in life.

♀ **Venus** The planet of love. Our ability to give and receive love and to feel happiness or lack of harmony. Our artistic taste. What we *like* or *dislike* in life.

♂ **Mars** The selfish side of our nature. The way in which we desire things for our own needs. To some extent, our aggressiveness. Also the 'male' side of our nature. In women, Mars can represent the man in their lives, just as Venus can represent the ideal woman in a man's horoscope. How we express *anger* in life.

♃ **Jupiter** Our good nature – the side that is generous, magnanimous and cheerful, or slapdash, wasteful and over-confident. Represents our ability to enlarge the scope of our interests. How we wish to *expand* in life.

♄ **Saturn** Our bad nature – the side that wants to restrict life and keep it under control. At best, our self-discipline and self-respect as well as moral courage and standards in life. At worst, our puritanical outlook on life and our ability to be over-cautious. How we *limit* life.

♅ **Uranus** The planet of disruption and revolution. The side of our nature that wants to break out of a rut, explore and try something new. Sometimes this is creatively inventive – at other times, it can be shocking and outrageous. How we are *original* in life.

♆ **Neptune** The planet of fantasy. The side of our nature that wants to escape from reality into the worlds of imagination.

The sensitive, vulnerable side of our nature – and also the self-deceptive side at times. How we *rise above* life.

♇   **Pluto** The furthermost planet of the solar system and one of the most mysterious. The side of our nature that needs to make complete breaks with the past – turning over a new leaf, disposing of unwanted ideas, burying feelings in the unconscious mind and – at times – allowing repressed emotions to flood back into everyday consciousness. How we make *fundamental changes* in life.

These planets are just as much the 'characters' of this book as the Royal Family itself. Each one of us is a 'family' of planets, and just as any family has its strengths and weaknesses, with one member possibly dominant over the rest, or another as the black sheep, so in our own horoscope can one planet stand out from the remainder or another fail to live up to its potential.

Each of us has a fatherly side to our nature, and in astrology this is represented by the position of the Sun. Fatherliness means responsibility for the whole family: earning money to pay for all its needs, giving leadership and direction to the family.

Motherliness, on the other hand, is represented by the Moon. Mother plays a more immediate role in the family circle; it is her feelings and moods and influence that affect the day-to-day running of the household, and so the Moon in astrology refers to our ordinary inner emotions: our habits, our sympathies, our response to life.

Mercury is the youngster of this 'family' of planets: its eyes and ears, aware of everything in the neighbourhood, cracking jokes, dreaming up super ideas, but lacking experience and wisdom. If Mercury is strong in your birth-chart, you are a quick-witted and perhaps reckless individual who finds it hard to grow up.

Venus is his elder sister, the sexually aware adolescent girl with few interests beyond her personal happiness. She does no work, has no intellectual ideas – just prettifies herself in the mirror and has a blazing love–hate relationship with her other brother, Mars, the rough teenager who is full of aggression and physical energy and competitiveness. So, if Venus is prominent in your horoscope, you cannot help being an agreeable, somewhat vain individual. If

Mars is strong, then you are active and a bit irascible. If they are both strong, you have a sex nature of large appetite.

Just as Venus and Mars are really a pair, so are the next planets, Jupiter and Saturn. Uncle Jove (Jupiter) is the free-and-easy fellow who breezes into the house with tales of his adventures; he expands their vision of the outside world. Grandfather (Saturn) is the crotchety old man who grumbles all the time – but in a family crisis he has wise advice from his wealth of experience.

The remaining three planets are not really relatives at all, but

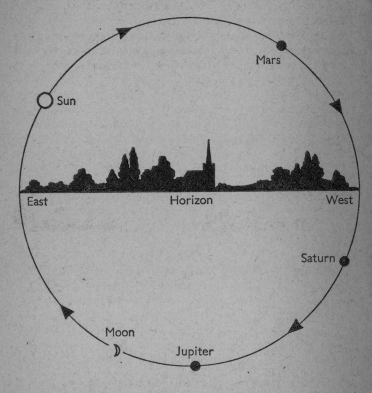

Figure 1 The Zodiac, along which the Sun, Moon and planets are placed, is constantly on the move, rising above the eastern horizon and sinking below the west.

raw natural forces that shake the household out of its rut. Lightning (Uranus), flood (Neptune) and earthquake (Pluto) would be apt descriptions of them!

Now you must begin to understand how these planets play their part in astrology. Picture a giant bicycle wheel circling clockwise through the sky, following the path of the Sun as it rises in the east, climbs high towards south and then, after noon, slips down to the west. That's one half of the wheel – the remainder is beneath the earth, of course – and this wheel, known as the Zodiac, revolves round and round, day after day, with the Sun, Moon and planets roughly aligned to its rim.

So the whole solar system swings round every twenty-four hours. But all the time the various celestial bodies are shifting their position. One moment the Sun will be to the right of a

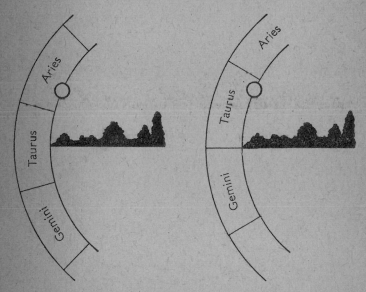

Figure 2 Although all starry objects keep moving anti-clockwise, they gradually 'slip back' in their positions. One morning the Sun may lie towards the end of Aries. At the same time the following week, the Sun rises above the same horizon, this time in the Zodiac sign of Gemini.

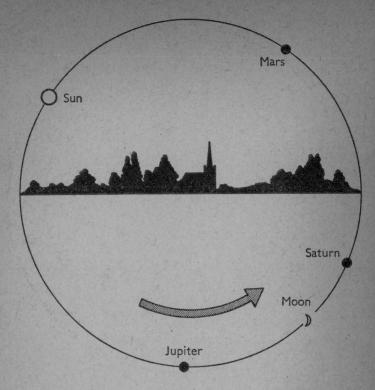

Figure 3 This 'slipping back' is slow, except in the case of the Moon. A week later than Figure 1, the Moon has shifted from a square aspect to the Sun (90°) to an opposition (180°).

bicycle spoke, so to speak, and the next moment it will have moved to the left. The Moon is the fastest of all, while the slowest is the most distant from Earth, Pluto. Every so often, two or more planets will get into line with each other, and when this happens an *aspect* is formed. The most powerful aspect is a *conjunction*, when the planets are side by side in the sky. Then comes an *opposition*, when, not surprisingly, they are opposite each other, and a *square*, when they are 90 degrees apart, and a *trine*, when they are 120 degrees apart. There are plenty more, but you needn't

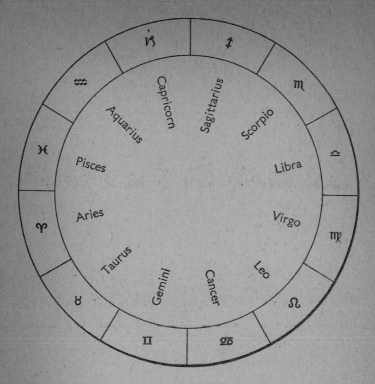

Figure 4 The Zodiac signs run in anti-clockwise order from Aries to Pisces. Each sign has its own symbol.

worry about them now. All you need to know is that when an aspect is formed, there's a strong communications link established between the particular planets concerned. When Venus and Mars are side by side in a conjunction, they merge their qualities . . . like a marriage. When they're in opposition, it's still a marriage . . . but a rather spiteful one. Planetary aspects will be mentioned a certain amount in this book, because they have a deeply significant role in astrology and therefore in the psychological make-up of the Royal Family.

Now our bicycle wheel, or Zodiac, is divided into the famous twelve segments known as the *signs of the Zodiac*. A Zodiac sign, in other words, is a sector of sky; and, if a particular planet is occupying that sector at the moment of birth, then 'Mercury is in Libra', it is said, or 'Venus lies in Sagittarius'. Each of these positions has a special meaning, depending on the planet and the sign involved. The normal Zodiac personal qualities associated with each month of the year are really interpretations of 'Sun in Aquarius' or 'Sun in Pisces', for of course the Sun spends about a month in each Zodiac sign.

Here are the broad characteristics of the Zodiac signs, together with the dates of the month when people are said to be 'born under' a particular sign. Each sign is described more fully in the book under each individual royal personality, so this is simply a summary. You will notice that each sign has a drawn symbol which is used in all the horoscopes in this book. There are also the well-known word-symbols such as the Ram, the Bull and the Heavenly Twins. No one knows exactly how these symbols originated. Some people say that the constellation of stars that long ago corresponded with each Zodiac sector of sky forms the outline of a Lion for Leo, say, or an Archer for Sagittarius. Other people, myself included, feel that each symbol has an inner significance for the Zodiac sign concerned, and several of these are explained later in the book.

Each Zodiac sign also has one of four Elements assigned to it: Earth, Air, Fire or Water. Here the symbolism is simple. All the Earth signs have a down-to-earth quality to them. The Air signs are breezy . . . or sometimes long-winded. The Fire signs burn with passion and enthusiasm and sometimes scorch other people with their anger. The Water signs are moist with sympathy, flowing with emotion . . . and often wet with indecision!

♒ **Aquarius** (21 Jan–18 Feb). Cool, calm, rational. Likes to be unshockable. Dispassionate about life, somewhat independent, keen on personal liberty. Good at observing life, not always a willing participant. Symbol: the Water Carrier. Element: Air.

♓ **Pisces** (19 Feb–20 Mar). Dreamy, sensitive, easily hurt. Very adaptable, eager to please, needing love and support from others. Absent-minded at times, imaginative, susceptible to the influence of others. Symbol: the Fish. Element: Water.

♈ **Aries** (21 Mar–20 Apr). Ardent, active, competitive. Very 'physical', respecting the facts rather than fancies. Brave, sometimes insensitive, argumentative, uncomplicated. Friendly but brusque. Symbol: the Ram. Element: Fire.

♉ **Taurus** (21 Apr–21 May). Stolid, down-to-earth, practical. Self-centred but still generous and hospitable. Artistic, appreciates the value of money! Very sociable. Stubborn at times, but full of commonsense. Symbol: the Bull. Element: Earth.

♊ **Gemini** (22 May–21 June). Lively, versatile, communicative. Quick-witted and adaptable. Interested in learning. A bit sly and two-faced at times. Very sociable. Finds it hard to grow up. Apt to be restless, veering from one extreme to the other. Symbol: the Twins. Element: Air.

♋ **Cancer** (22 June–22 July). Sensitive and defensive in outlook. Home-loving, private, very emotional. Very protective towards loved ones – but likes to be thanked for everything! The motherly sort, cowardly but tenacious. Symbol: the Crab. Element: Water.

♌ **Leo** (23 July–23 Aug). Warm, outgoing, self-confident. Likes to be leader. Must be admired by others. Can be too vain and pompous. Drawn to the recreational side of life. Sociable, but likes to be centre of attention. Symbol: the Lion. Element: Fire.

♍ **Virgo** (24 Aug–22 Sept). Analytical and efficient. Tidy-minded. Can be a worrier, especially about health. A bit narrow-minded at times, and can lack charm and warmth. Pure-minded, with high standards in life. Symbol: the Virgin. Element: Earth.

♎ **Libra** (23 Sept–23 Oct). Charming, amiable and soft-hearted. Can be very indecisive. Artistic and tasteful. Needs company in order to be happy. Takes the balanced, middle-of-the-road point of view. Symbol: the Pair of Scales. Element: Air.

♏ **Scorpio** (24 Oct–22 Nov). Intense, determined and single-minded. Needs to live up to own high standards. Can be jealous and vindictive. Keeps cool in a crisis. Very emotional, but shows little on the surface. Symbol: the Scorpion. Element: Water.

♐ **Sagittarius** (23 Nov–21 Dec). Carefree, adventurous and easy-going. Independent and self-reliant, but still friendly with others. Good sense of justice. Can be slapdash at times. Has wide vision and a desire to travel. Symbol: the Archer. Element: Fire.

♑ **Capricorn** (22 Dec–20 Jan). Hard-headed, tough and realistic. Can survive, but feels self-pity. Good with money. High moral sense, but not very relaxed or 'giving'. Ambitious and keen to play a public role. Symbol: the Goat. Element: Earth.

It's a comparatively easy job to put planets and Zodiac signs together to create the psychological building-blocks that are the fabric of an individual's personality. Thus Venus (love) in Gemini (lively, versatile) means a free-and-easy romantic disposition with a variety-seeking appetite in love, and it's no surprise to learn that King Henry VIII had this configuration in his birth-chart!

Obviously there are clashes in nearly every horoscope, because very few people are a model of harmony and peace within themselves. In Henry's case, for instance, his Sun (inner character) lay in Cancer (home-loving), so he was basically a family man who longed for a quiet domestic life. If you recall, he married each of his six wives because he desperately wanted a male heir that would ensure the continuance of his *family*. True, he was also a promiscuous man, but this often caused him agonies of conscience.

We have looked at planets, aspects and Zodiac signs. Now we must understand two very important parts of astrology, the *Midheaven* and *Ascendant*. Let's go back to that vast imaginary bicycle wheel spinning clockwise round our sky day after day. At

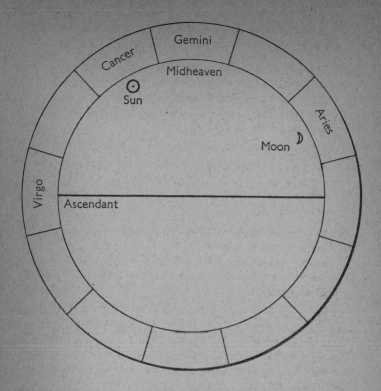

Figure 5 The important factors in Henry VIII's horoscope: the Ascendant in Virgo, Sun in Cancer, Midheaven in Gemini, and Moon in Aries.

the moment of birth, the wheel stops, so to speak, and becomes the circle of the horoscope. The upper semicircle is the sky overhead, while the lower semicircle is that part of the heavens underneath the Earth at the time.

If you think of the horoscope as a clockface, the Ascendant is situated at nine o'clock and the Midheaven at roughly twelve o'clock. The Ascendant is the part of the Zodiac rising above the eastern horizon at the moment of the baby's birth; and the Midheaven is the part of the Zodiac lying due south at that time. The Ascendant is sometimes known as the Rising sign, for obvious reasons. People get muddled because the cardinal points are different from those in the compass; remember that the horoscope is a map of the solar system viewed by someone facing due south at the birthplace, with east on the left and west on the right.

The Ascendant, Sun-sign, Moon-sign and Midheaven are the most important parts of anyone's horoscope. Together they give a convincing thumbnail sketch of the individual's personality. The Ascendant gives the outer temperament of the person, while the Midheaven tells us about his destiny in the world – that is, the kind of person he would like to become.

If we stick with Henry VIII, we find that he had a *Virgo Ascendant*, so at first glance he appeared a worrier and a critic, finding fault with other people and trying to get things perfect. Certainly he was always finding fault with his wives, and he was a sharp critic of the Roman Catholic church.

With his *Gemini Midheaven*, his destiny was to be restless, moving from one activity to the next without a great sense of permanence in his life. He also aspired to be a scholar, which is a very Geminian characteristic.

His *Sun in Cancer* made him a crab-like figure, tough on the outside but sensitive in his heart of hearts. And his *Moon in Aries* gave him an emotional temperament which was hot, fiery and irascible.

There remains one further set of factors that need to be taken into consideration in an astrological interpretation. These are the *Houses*. The bicycle wheel can be divided into Zodiac signs, as we've seen; but also into Houses, which are simply another set of twelve segments, this time starting from a different point on the circle, namely the Ascendant. Think of the clockface again, with the Ascendant at nine o'clock. The Houses run anti-clockwise from this point, so the First House lies between eight and nine, the Second House between seven and eight, the Third House between six and seven, right round to the Twelfth House between nine and ten. All very confusing, but it's easy once you've got the hang of it.

Any planet in a particular House has a special meaning in addi-

tion to its position in its Zodiac sign. These are the meanings of
each House:

First House Very important. Any planet here has a vivid effect
on one's outer temperament. Oliver Cromwell, *Pluto in First
House*: a very intense man with a strong sense of destiny.

Second House To do with money and possessions. Charles I,
Moon in Second House: it was his emotional attachment to the
royal revenues that brought about the Civil War in Britain.

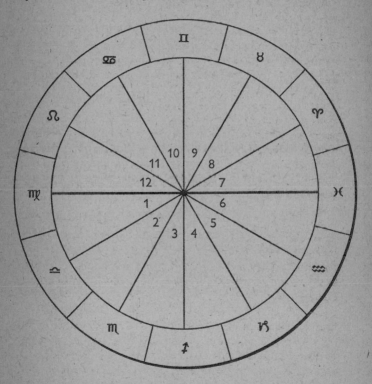

Figure 6 The Houses in Henry's horoscope, starting just below the
Ascendant and running anti-clockwise.

Third House To do with education and the communication of ideas. Charles Dickens, England's greatest novelist, *Mercury in Third House*: great facility in writing, talking and teaching.

Fourth House To do with home, family, inherited characteristics. Her Majesty the Queen, *Sun in Fourth House*: a deeply conservative, home-oriented woman.

Fifth House To do with fun, recreations, children – all the relaxing, creative side of life. William Blake, artist and poet, *Jupiter in Fifth House*: versatile in many artistic fields.

Sixth House To do with health and one's attitude to work. Karl Marx, *Uranus in Sixth House*: a revolutionary outlook on working conditions.

Seventh House Very important. Any planet here has a direct effect on one's ability to get on with others – especially in one's marriage. Mary Queen of Scots, *Saturn in Seventh House*: disappointment in her married life.

Eighth House To do with the basic mysteries – life, death and life-after-death. One's ability to solve big problems. Harry Houdini, the escapologist, *Uranus in Eighth House*: a man with unconventional ways of getting out of difficulties!

Ninth House To do with travel and the broadening of the mind. Elizabeth I, *Sun in Ninth House*: a woman wanting to explore the world and expand the power and prestige of England.

Tenth House To do with one's career and desire to be important in life. Henry VIII, *Jupiter in Tenth House*: successful in his job as King.

Eleventh House To do with friends, clubs and associations of people. Joan of Arc, *Mars in Eleventh House*: able to play a martial role (i.e. as a soldier) among other people.

Twelfth House To do with one's private, unconscious life, and the ability to keep one's thoughts secret from others. Cardinal Richelieu, *Mars in Twelfth House*: energetic in keeping secrets from others.

Each House, like an individual country, has its own Head of State known as a *ruler*, and this is one of the planets in the horoscope. Rulership is determined by the Zodiac sign on the *cusp* of the House. The cusp of the First House, going back to our clockface, is nine o'clock, the cusp of the Second House is eight o'clock, and so on round the circle. So, in Fig. 6, nine o'clock points towards Virgo, so the ruler of the First House is the ruling planet of Virgo, which, according to the table below, is Mercury. This First House ruler is very important in anyone's chart; it's said, in fact, to be the ruler (or dominant influence) of the whole horoscope.

Sign	Ruling planet
Aries	Mars
Taurus	Venus
Gemini	Mercury
Cancer	Moon
Leo	Sun
Virgo	Mercury
Libra	Venus
Scorpio	Pluto
Sagittarius	Jupiter
Capricorn	Saturn
Aquarius	Uranus
Pisces	Neptune

Naturally, you can still enjoy this book without understanding all that much about astrology. If you are interested in the technical side of astrology, you should know that I work using the Equal House Tropical Zodiac system, and that all birth-data given here is based on local time or Greenwich Mean Time.

To make them more readable to people new to astrology, I have not shown the exact planetary positions in the royal horoscopes throughout this book. The complete planetary data is included in the Appendix. If you want to analyse these charts in greater depth, see my book *Astrology for Everyone* (Hodder Causton).

Part One **Past**

Victoria and Albert

Our accustomed picture of Queen Victoria – that pale, mournful face topped by a lace cap, that bulky figure dressed in blackest crinoline – is true of her old age. But the real Victoria, shown in her private diaries and her personal horoscope, is a much more complex, likeable creature – by turns gay, dramatic, high-principled, naïve, obstinate and industrious.

Earlier astrologers, born in the closing stages of the Victorian Age, could not believe that she had Gemini rising. No, they asserted, the time of birth must be wrong, probably by a quarter of an hour or more. Stodgy, boring, conventional old Victoria must have had Taurus, the bull, as her Ascendant; she was so bovine herself.

To me, however, Victoria is pure, unadulterated Geminian stock. She was born on 24 May 1819 in Kensington Palace, at 4.15 a.m. This makes her a double Gemini, with the Sun and Ascendant in this sign.

Gemini is the sign of the heavenly twins, one of whom lived in heaven and the other on earth. More than most people, Geminians veer between opposites – good and bad, optimism and melancholy, truth and expediency. They are fidgety, restless people forever changing their minds, darting from one interest to the next, jumping in will-o'-the-wisp fashion from idea to idea, rarely settling down to one proper job of work. They are quick and sharp, alert to detail, marvellous at picking up moods and thoughts, often mimicking people without realizing what they are doing, and have been compared with Cockney spivs, chirpy house sparrows and, most appositely of all, with monkeys.

It's easy to miss the more serious side of the Geminian character, the heavenly as opposed to the all-too-earthly aspect of their nature. Gemini represents the thirst for knowledge, the

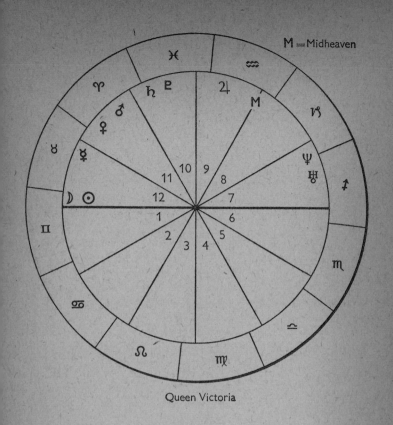

Queen Victoria

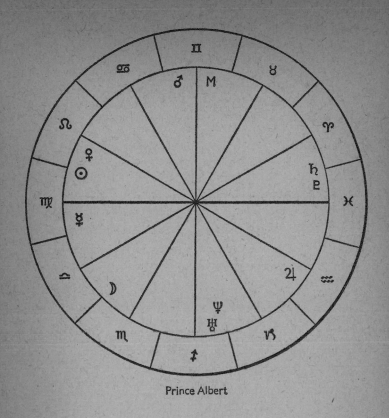

Prince Albert

desire to stay in touch with the world. The planet most closely linked with this Zodiac sign is Mercury, who in classical mythology was the messenger of the gods. Geminians love being messengers, or, better still, telephone operators, taking in-coming messages from a wide range of sources and happily passing on information, ideas, gossip, to whomever wants to listen. And, like all voices at the switchboard, you cannot put a face to them. Gemini is the sign of a thousand faces, a thousand different appearances to suit a multitude of differing circumstances. With Gemini, things are never as they seem. Behind humour there is profundity. The wisest character in a Shakespeare play is usually the Fool, who is a dramatic representation of Gemini.

What has all this to do with Queen Victoria? Let us look at the Geminian qualities in her character.

Victoria, in the first place, was certainly a handful of characters rolled into one. She assumed five major roles in her lifetime. First the shy, repressed child cloistered by her mother, the Duchess of Kent, while she was groomed for monarchy; then, when she came to the throne at the age of eighteen and was free of maternal restrictions, the exuberant young woman, fiery young monarch, and adoring young wife to Albert. This was gradually followed by the somewhat reluctant mother and submissive spouse to an increasingly dominant husband. Abruptly, in early middle age, she became the nonplussed widow beset by political problems; and, finally, in the last twenty years of her life, the Mother of the British Empire, head of European royalty, the symbolic fount of worldwide power.

Her appearance was Geminian. True, the basic bone structure was plumply Hanoverian, but her short inches, her lightness of step, the cock of her head as she listened to court gossip and the peals of laughter whenever she heard something amusing – these are the signs of the lively Gemini spirit. How she loved humour! She was keenly awake to wit in others, and in her younger days made many sharply funny remarks herself. The notorious retort of 'We are not amused' is not typically Victorian.

True to her Geminian nature, she was a magnificent letter-writer and diarist. All over Europe, friends and relatives, especially her beloved daughter Vicky and uncle Leopold, received fat pages of script, often weekly, sometimes daily, covered in her near-illegible scrawl. Victoria's letters are full of drama. She had a fine insight into human character and, though no great stylist herself, revealed the essence of her personality more directly and vividly than many a more accomplished writer. Like a child eager to convey her message, she could not leave words alone. She had to emphasize, put letters in capitals or italics, underline sentences several times so that no one would doubt her meaning.

She had many other Geminian characteristics – she loved using her hands, for instance, to gesticulate when talking, to play the piano or sketch from nature – but what still seems wrong, at first glance, is that Victoria was not the easy-going, ever-youthful individual, deceptive and even a bit sly, suggested by the Gemini image. On the contrary, she combined some Geminian qualities with much strength of character, persistence and indomitability.

The reason why Victoria's character contains so many more elements than one single Zodiac sign lies in the positions of the Sun and Moon. Not only were they side by side in the sky when she was born, meaning that there was a New Moon that morning; they were almost exactly on the eastern horizon, in the most important part of the sky in anyone's horoscope. So the three crucial elements in astrology – Sun, Moon and Ascendant – were all closely in conjunction.

This means that her outer temperament (Ascendant), inner character (Sun) and emotional disposition (Moon) were all interwoven, eager to express themselves, almost elbowing each other aside in their need to be manifested in her everyday life.

It means, too, that Victoria was almost a 'family' in herself. People born at dawn, with the Sun in the east, are solar individuals. They radiate warmth, energy, charisma. They get things done. They adopt, in effect, a 'fatherly' role towards people around them, giving orders, taking responsibility, making their world revolve around them.

In the same way, anyone, like Victoria, born with the Moon rising above the eastern horizon is a lunar person – yes, at times a loony person, too! She could throw a fit of hysterics, and suffered a nervous breakdown after the death of her mother. The Moon, of course, represents the maternal side of life. Apart from her own numerous offspring, the whole British people became, in effect, Victoria's children. She was known as the Mother of the Empire. She had a deeply cherishing attitude towards life – towards children in particular, but animals too, the countryside, anybody with whom she had personal contact. Her many homes, from Osborne on the Isle of Wight to Scotland's Balmoral, were where she felt happiest. Throughout her life she travelled little, and during the last forty years she rarely left her own grounds at all, except to travel to the next castle, palace or country house.

Already a 'father' figure and 'mother' figure, Victoria was also a 'child', due to the pervading influence of Gemini, the most youthful and adolescent of all the Zodiac signs. In short, her personality smacks of a deeply ancient symbol in human consciousness: the trinity, the nuclear family. No wonder that she was revered in her lifetime as a massive, inevitable presence. No wonder that her death, in 1901, marked the end of an era. Still today, Victoria is a milestone by which we measure history. This triple conjunction in Gemini, which is the crux of her astrological character, is a rare event. It lasts no more than twenty minutes, once a year.

What is fascinating, when studying Victoria's character, is to realize how inadequately she was provided with family life in her early years – and how this shaped her attitudes towards life. Her father died when she was less than a year old, leaving her in the hands of a mother who did not truly understand her. 'I don't believe Ma ever really loved me,' she once said. So her childhood was a lonely affair, without the company of other children.

Suddenly, in her late teens, she became father, mother and child all at once, when she ascended the Throne, met Albert and became a liberated young woman. But all her life she was in need of the right father figure to replace her actual dead parent. At first there was Melbourne, her worldly, affable Prime Minister during the first years of her reign. Later there would be the dashing Disraeli and the sombre Scotch gillie, John Brown. But the most important man in her life, naturally, was her husband Albert.

The marriage was arranged by her mother and uncle Leopold, with Victoria's consent, of course. The cousins met when Victoria was seventeen, and she thanked Leopold for 'the prospect of *great* happiness you have given me in the person of dear Albert'. Two years later, the prospect became reality. The most celebrated and devoted royal marriage had begun.

To modern eyes Albert is an unsympathetic character. Albert the Good, Victoria called him, and his so-called virtues of rectitude, discipline and lofty idealism are not much admired in our slack, cynical times. But whatever age nurtured him, astrology shows that he would still have been a cold, intelligent prig.

He was born, the second son of Duchess Louise of Saxe-Coburg-Saalfeld, shortly after daybreak on 26 August, in the same year as Victoria. His mother, who smothered him in love in his early years, left him at the age of five, and thereafter he lived in a world of men, disliking women and often playing hideous schoolboy tricks on them. He was a sickly child and remained a hypochondriac all his life. But he had a brain, a good one, and through diligent tutorage he became a first-class man of reason. He loved ideas, schemes, theories, practical efforts – but despised human beings. He was, in short, the worst kind of Virgo individual.

Virgo's symbol, of course, is the Virgin, but this has little to do with sexual inexperience. Virgo is concerned with purity, the kind of purity that results from a long process of refinement. Think of a combine harvester moving steadily through a field of corn, reaping the crop, separating the grain from the ch'ff, storing the inner goodness and discarding the straw and husk. This is the instinctive Virgoan approach to life. People born under this sign place a wary, critical eye on everything around them. They cannot take anything for granted; always it must be examined, checked, queried and, if necessary, rejected. Only the worthwhile, the useful, is retained.

At best, they are the salt of the earth – the natural craftsmen and technicians of this world, using their skills to transform physical resources into civilized artefacts. But people like this, with a scientific turn of mind, run the risk of being too desiccated in their personal life. They think of other people as machines to be controlled, ordered about, put through their paces. Albert was incredibly strict with his children, putting them through rigorous courses of education that might have suited ideal, theoretical children, but not real flesh-and-blood ones. He was as sympathetic as . . . a combine harvester.

Poor Albert, poor Virgo! He stands today as a terrible advertisement for this modest, unoffending Zodiac sign. He had no sense of humour, for instance, but, realizing how much these foreigners, the English, relish laughter, he solemnly learnt jokes and endlessly repeated them, always being the first to laugh himself. His real brand of wit was sarcasm, at which he excelled, and gave a bellow of delighted laughter if anyone suffered physical pain, like slipping on a banana skin.

Just as Victoria was a double Gemini, Albert was a double Virgo, with the added emphasis of the planet Mercury, which is the ruler of Virgo, placed in this sign in the First House.

This First House, just below the eastern horizon, is like the threshold. Any planet there is quickly noticed by passers-by and is the first to greet visitors. In Albert's case, the mercurial qualities – brains, communicativeness, a love of paperwork – were ever-present in his character and plain for everyone to see. This planet here also made him a much more egocentric individual than most Virgoan people. He thought highly of himself – and not much of anyone else.

So this able, conscientious, rational man became Prince Consort to an exceedingly strong-minded, naïve Queen whose natural sense of decorum was the sometimes ill-fitting lid on a cauldron of fiery emotions. Albert's first aim was to rob her of power. The great link between them, astrologically speaking, was the fact that his Midheaven lay in conjunction with her Sun, Moon and Ascendant in the early degrees of Gemini. This part of the sky, in other words, was exactly due south of Coburg when Albert was born.

The Midheaven, in anyone's chart, represents the way that person squares up to life. It is his destiny, his place in the world – and, in a man's case certainly, this means primarily his career. Albert's career, it follows, *was* Queen Victoria – looking after her, coping with her moods, ultimately taking over from her.

It was a painful process for both of them. In the early years of their marriage, Victoria, conscious of her unique role as monarch, would let Albert interfere little, or not at all, with affairs of state. So he took command of the royal household, ousting Victoria's confidante, Baroness Lehzen, from her role as governess, supervising the children's care and upbringing, transforming the royal finances from parlous debt to thriving prosperity.

Gradually, as Victoria accepted Albert as a true, trustworthy father figure, she yielded increasingly more royal duties to his care. One reason why, after Albert's death, she took so long to return to even nominal work as Queen was that she had lost touch with administration. Albert had taken over.

He took over much of her personality, too – another way in which his Midheaven methodically gobbled up her Sun, Moon and Ascendant. He took away some of her buoyancy and high spirits, much of her humour, and probably a part of her vitality, too. Victoria was rarely ill, Albert nearly always. As a child he was chesty and croupy and perennially sleepy; as an adult he was tortured by rheumatism, wracked with stomach aches, pallid with worry, nerves, migraine, sudden fevers, melancholia and insomnia. With his Sun tucked away in the Twelfth House, he lacked physical stamina. Worse, he lacked the will to live. Anyone with the Sun in this position, just above the eastern horizon, is quite a shy, withdrawn individual with a powerful introverted streak. This was the contradiction in Albert's character. On the one hand, he was the energetic, scholarly administrator, driving himself to play a dominant part in the world. On the other, he was a recluse from ordinary real life. He had no close friends. He loved wild countryside such as he found in the forests of his childhood home in Germany and discovered in later life in the Scottish Highlands. He was an unfortunate ambiguity: a dreamer with no imagination, a martinet with no stamina. He drove himself to death.

Albert's demise is the most famous in English history, as it radically changed the Queen's character and dominated court life for the remaining forty years of her reign. Surely death, the ultimate in earthly events, can be foreseen, astrologers are often asked. Indian astrologers claim that it can, but I am not so sure. It depends what kind of death, in what circumstances, to whom – and with what results to those people affected by the death.

Victoria, as we know, suffered an all-consuming trauma when Albert caught infectious fever and died on 14 December 1861. Her horoscope, surely, should show this grievous turning-point.

There are two principal means of using astrology to foretell the future – or, in this case, to anticipate the past. The first is called *directions*, the second – and more common – method is known as *transits*.

Directions couldn't be simpler. The Zodiac circle is divided into 360 segments known as degrees, and each planet in a horoscope lies in a particular degree. Jupiter, in Victoria's chart, lies in the seventeenth degree of Aquarius, for example, while Saturn lies in the twenty-ninth degree of the following sign, Pisces. There are thirty degrees in each sign, so this means there are forty-two degrees between Jupiter and Saturn (twelve in Aquarius, twenty-nine in Pisces). According to this system of directions, planets can be mentally moved around the Zodiac – one degree for each year of life. When an important aspect occurs in this way between one planet and another, we should expect a suitable event, coinciding with the type of planets involved, to occur in the person's life.

So the forty-two degrees between Jupiter and Saturn means there would be a Jupiter–Saturn conjunction in Victoria's horoscope when she was forty-two years old – in 1861, the year of Albert's death. Her optimism and cheerfulness, represented by Jupiter, would become clouded over by the sadness and limitations indicated by Saturn.

We can be more precise about this. Marriage is indicated in astrology by the Seventh House, the sector of sky just above the western horizon. What's called the cusp of this House – the division between the sixth and seventh Houses, in fact – lies in Sagittarius. The ruling planet of Sagittarius is Jupiter. So Jupiter is the planet representing the Queen's marriage. When Jupiter meets Saturn, in 1861, the marriage runs into trouble.

We can be even more precise. Death is indicated by the Eighth House. Its cusp lies in Capricorn. The ruling planet of Capricorn is Saturn. So when Jupiter (marriage) meets Saturn (death), the inference is plain.

There is another important direction in Victoria's horoscope in the same year. Pluto is forty-two degrees apart from Mercury, so these two planets form a conjunction in 1861. Pluto represents trauma, crisis, a difficult turning-point. Mercury stands for mental stability, besides being the ruler of her whole chart. This Pluto–Mercury conjunction is an exact astrological symbol for the mental cataclysm that engulfed Victoria when she became widowed.

The other way of making predictions about the future is the use of transits. By this system we compare the planetary positions in the sky at a particular time with the positions in the horoscope, and if there are any aspects in force, they have a bearing on events and moods at that time.

When Albert shuffled off his mortal coil, Victoria was certainly suffering. Despite the fact that transits are a completely different mathematical system to directions, very similar aspects are made. Jupiter, which we know is the indicator of the Queen's marriage, was placed in the sky exactly opposite Pluto in her horoscope, which corresponds with crisis and emotional turmoil. And Pluto itself, in that December sky of 1861, was stationed at the same exact Zodiac degree as Mercury in her chart – so once again we find a Pluto–Mercury conjunction in force at this crucial time. When astrologers see the same message written two different ways, they pay attention.

It was all a ghastly shock to Victoria, who didn't believe in illness and resolutely insisted on Albert taking wintry walks on her arm while the typhoid fever raged inside him. Albert himself had known he would die for years. He told Victoria: 'I do not cling to life. You do; but I set no store by it . . . I am sure, if I had a severe illness, I should give up at once.' Which he did. Neptune, the link between conscious and unconscious states, was subtly at work in his horoscope. It was exactly opposite the two most difficult planets in astrology – Saturn and Pluto – which lay in his Seventh House, to do with his marriage. Whatever history may say, it had not been an easy relationship for the Prince to bear; indeed, with these two planets affecting the issue, it had been the heavy cross he had been forced to bear through the best part of his adult life. Now, with Neptune washing away the traces, the marriage was no more.

Other, more precise, configurations give the whole story:
Saturn = Mercury/Uranus (separating from others),
Jupiter = Mars/Neptune (congestion of the lungs).

It remains a mystery why history has believed Victoria that theirs was a consummately happy union. They quarrelled a great deal. She, with the two sexy planets in the ardent sign of Aries, was a passionate woman, he merely a consenting mate. 'Really, I do not think it *possible* for anyone in the world to be *happier*, or AS happy as I am,' she scribbled off to uncle Leopold on the first day of her honeymoon. Albert's reaction, to his old tutor in Coburg, was more circumspect: 'The change in my life is very great, but I am beginning to adapt myself.' Both were constantly — and quite unnecessarily — jealous of each other, for Prince Virgo was a virgin at marriage and never looked at another woman, while Queen Gemini, who certainly fancied other men and was in love with two of her Prime Ministers, had the Geminian gift to flirt without needing to express it in physical love. If Albert or Victoria had ever been unfaithful, the marriage would not have lasted. He was too pure, she too highly-strung.

Astrology shows that temperamentally they were not suited. She needed a more lusty, extrovert, laughing husband who would set her giggling and smack her bottom when she started her hysterics. With some other man as Consort, we should have avoided all the gloomy latter half of the Victorian era. We should have had a lively, natural, more mature Edward VII. The world would have been a nicer place.

Three other men played significant roles in Victoria's life. The first was Lord Melbourne, the urbane Prime Minister who taught the young Queen statecraft and much else besides in the first years of her reign. He had led a hellbent life, with two marriages and two divorces behind him — one to the notorious Caroline Lamb who appeared naked on dinner tables and slashed her wrists in public before clearing off with Lord Byron. But in June 1837, when Victoria came to the throne, Melbourne became a changed man: discreet, dignified, deferential, spending many hours a day with the Queen, between four and six on average, riding together in the park, dining together, chatting late into the night in her private drawing-room at Windsor. If he was called back to

London, she cried: 'I am very sorry to lose him even for one night.'

Melbourne was born on 15 March 1779. As a Piscean he was a solitary and thoughtful man and called himself a 'quietist', someone who hated arguments and political warfare. Pisceans are among the gentlest of people, but they can also be indecisive. Stockmar, a friend of Albert's, called him 'weak and careless', but Melbourne didn't like Albert either, and urged Victoria not to marry him. At times there was talk of Victoria and Melbourne marrying. Certainly they were 'in love' – he with a sweet, young, naïve girl who was suddenly Queen, she with this 58-year-old statesman who could converse brilliantly on all kinds of ideas she had never heard discussed at the Kensington Palace schoolroom.

To some extent it was a father–daughter relationship (his Sun is close to her Saturn). In another way they were lovers, though never physically (there is a close contact between her Venus, representing love, and his Mars, representing his manhood). But mainly they obeyed the call of destiny, this statesman and young queen. Most notably of all in their horoscopes, his Pluto, signifying that part of his nature that is fated and ineluctable, exactly conjoins her Midheaven, symbolizing her career or place in the world. The literal meaning of this conjunction is 'the shaping of the individual' or 'people excelling in their profession'. Together, Victoria and Melbourne created that strong, enduring force known as Queen Victoria.

When Melbourne left office in the spring of 1839, Victoria was hysterical. 'The thought of ALL, ALL, my happiness being possibly at stake', she wrote in her diary, 'so completely overcame me that I burst into tears.' She was faced with dull, stolid Peel, just as later in life she was forced to alternate between worthy but oh-so-boring Mr Gladstone and the remarkable, ineffable Dizzy.

'Gladstone treats the Queen like a public department,' said Disraeli at one stage. 'I treat her like a woman.' Although she considered him, at first, as 'unprincipled, reckless, & not respectable' – and Albert agreed with her – once she was a widow she found her new Prime Minister an irresistible mixture of charm, style and oddity. People accused him of slyly manipulating a middle-aged woman who was infatuated with him – but, at the same time, a more prosaic monarch than Victoria would never have captured his high-flown imagination. In the nicest possible way, they deserved each other.

Disraeli was a Sagittarian by birth: a much more adventurous sign than dry Virgo and the polar opposite of Victoria's own sign of Gemini. But what gave the man his singular allure was the presence of three planets side by side with his Ascendant. Dizzy's trio was Venus, Jupiter and Neptune – what may be called the three 'feminine' planets, because they refer to the softer, more receptive qualities of personality rather than the hard, outgoing ones.

Venus is the planet of love, charm, beauty and artistic interests. Any man with Venus rising is a ladies' man, a man with imagination, a man who wants to please. Next comes Jupiter, the planet of optimism and success. Put Venus and Jupiter together on the Ascendant and you have a man of great appeal who can make friends quickly and easily, a man of considerable luck who sails through life without much difficulty. And add Neptune, the imaginative-plus factor in astrology, and you have Dizzy incarnate – the dandy, the romantic novelist, the deft politician harbouring visions of imperial glory to rival Xanadu in splendour. Dizzy! – who called Victoria his 'Faery Queen', who said that her gift of primroses to him meant that 'your Majesty's sceptre has touched the enchanted isle,' who wrote 'I love the Queen – perhaps the only person in this world left to me that I do love . . .' And she loved him in return. She was a true Geminian; she knew it was a fanciful charade, a game of love that heightened matters of State but never detracted from them.

In astrology the twelve Zodiac signs can be grouped into four divisions known as the Elements. Each sign is Fire, Air, Earth or Water. The first two, Fire and Air, are compatible, as they are both un-solid, un-earthbound, free to dart here and there without obeying the law of gravity. Victoria, being strongly Geminian, was an intensely Airy individual. Dizzy, with his Sagittarian Sun and Moon in Leo, was Fire. Fire consumes Air. They dance together. Poor Albert, with all that Virgo, was utterly Earth. So was the wretched Gladstone, with the Sun rising in Capricorn. No, what Victoria needed was Fire – to awaken her high spirits, to kindle her sexual interest, to set her imagination ablaze. And she found it, glowing like embers in a peasant's hearth, in John Brown.

John Brown was a Scottish gillie who had been chosen by the Prince Consort, in the first place, to serve the Queen when the Royal Family were at Balmoral. In 1864, when Victoria was just beginning to recover from Albert's death three years earlier, she summoned John Brown to London to become her personal attendant. From then, until his death nineteen years later, he became increasingly dominant in the Queen's life. He protected her from intrusions, supervised her day-to-day arrangements, and conversed with her more freely and bluntly than anyone else, including members of her family.

They all loathed him. It seemed against all sense and seemliness that Her Majesty, at the summit of the social order, should allow this rough drunkard of a servant so much influence and prestige. He lacked deference, which at least might have made his post as companion – well, just acceptable. But he was also rude and tactless and quarrelsome, particularly towards the Prince of Wales. And how he drank! Every so often he became so 'bashful', as it was called, that he could not attend to his duties. The Queen learnt never to question these absences. She turned a blind eye to many of his excesses, and would not hear a word spoken against the man. She sent him greetings cards 'from his true & devoted one', 'from his best friend'. And after his death, she wrote: 'I have lost my *dearest best* friend who no-one in *this World* can *ever* replace . . .'

Like Disraeli, John Brown was a Sagittarian. Like him, he had his Moon in another Fire sign, this time Aries. His Sun is just two signs away from her Jupiter, four away from her Mars. His Venus is exactly four signs away from her ruler Mercury. Best of all, his Mars conjoins her Jupiter, exactly as it should be between attentive husband and loving wife. For rumours there were a-plenty about Mrs John Brown. And who can blame people for gossiping – for wasn't the Queen closeted with Brown away at Osborne or Balmoral, where nobody could see them?

Certainly in the late 1860s, when rumours were at their height, Mars in the Queen's horoscope had moved by direction to be in conjunction with her Sun, Moon and Ascendant. This is likely to have corresponded with a quickening of her sensuality, though whether or not she expressed it in physical terms, however indirect, is a mystery that will never be fully solved.

John Brown, for his part, had a poignant configuration in his own horoscope which provides most of the answer. In one part of the sky were Venus and Neptune; opposite lay Saturn. The meaning of this aspect is 'romantic melancholy', as though Brown was bound to be disappointed by a love that could never be fulfilled.

If not as husband, then, why not as clairvoyant? Throughout this century there have been reports that John Brown, rugged and tipsy though he often was, happened also to be a natural medium. When Queen Victoria discovered this gift, she used John Brown as a psychic means to get in touch with her beloved dead Albert.

There is no real evidence that this was so. The only sector of Brown's horoscope suggesting a supernatural talent is the Venus–Neptune conjunction already mentioned, and it was far more likely to manifest itself as a fondness for strong spirits than ghostly ones.

Queen Victoria had to wait until 1901 before she was reunited with Albert the Good. On 22 January 1901, at 6.30 p.m., surrounded by children and grandchildren, a calmness suffused her face and she was gone. At that moment, the Sun and Mercury both lay in that part of the sky which was her Midheaven; her work was done, her destiny complete, and she could slip away from earthly life.

At her death, Jupiter had advanced by direction to be conjunct her Mercury. Jupiter, representing her marriage, had joined with Mercury, representing herself. Who can doubt that Albert, ever dutiful, was waiting to escort his bride on another honeymoon, in another country, leaving the earthly stage for Bertie?

Bertie and Alix

Bertie was kept waiting all his life. By her longevity, his mother kept him waiting to become King until he was nearly sixty years old. By her insouciant disregard for time, his wife kept him waiting, hour upon hour, for private appointments and public duties, much to his furious chagrin. And by his sheer Virgoan narrow-mindedness, his father kept him waiting all right – waiting to grow up, waiting to meet friends, waiting to join the army.

All these delays were terribly frustrating to a man with such exuberant love of life. But they are an integral part of his personality, for one of the great lessons of astrology is that the circumstances we encounter in life are as much a factor in our total identity as our individual personal qualities. We *are* the events that happen to us.

This is so clearly shown in Edward's horoscope. He was born at 10.48 on the morning of 9 November 1841, when the planet Saturn was almost exactly on the eastern horizon. Saturn in astrology signifies the limitations and disappointments in life. It is akin to the skeleton, the framework that cannot be altered, the structure that determines the overall shape of one's life. Anyone with Saturn rising, as Edward had, tends to lead a life beset with problems: there are frustrations at every turn; there is often loneliness, or at least a feeling that one cannot communicate one's difficulties to other people. Above all, the individual grows up too quickly, in the sense that he does not have a free-and-easy childhood. In Bertie's case, this meant living out his childhood in adult years, indulging himself for the deprivations of his youth.

Exactly square to Saturn in the east, in Edward's horoscope, is the Moon in the Tenth House, high in the southern sky. The Moon represents his family background in general, and his mother in particular. The Tenth House deals with his career. It follows that

47

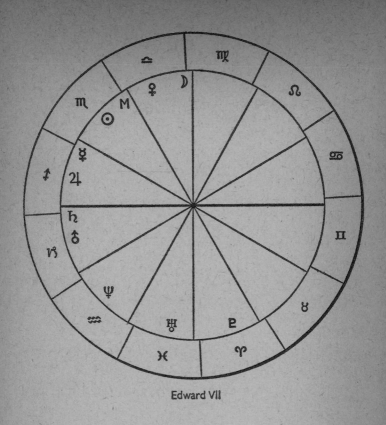

Edward VII

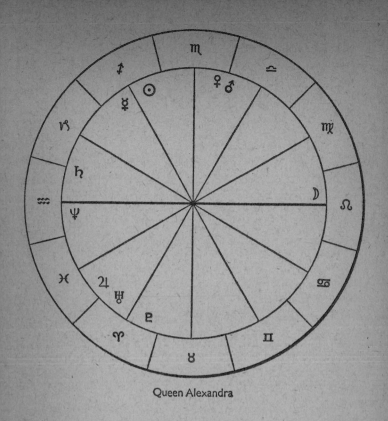

Queen Alexandra

Edward was very conscious of being part of a 'family business', and emotionally he needed to play a big role on the public stage. He was also conscious, right up until his sixtieth year, that his mother stood in the way of his career – not simply by preventing him from being King, but frustrating his every effort to be a worthy Prince of Wales. Victoria was the boss and found it difficult to delegate responsibility to anyone. (To this extent, with the Sun and Moon rising, she was a fierce egocentric.) In particular, she found herself unable to trust her son Bertie. Quite deliberately she thwarted him – and this Moon–Saturn square aspect is the clear astrological indication of the deep *anxiety* that existed between mother and son. Bertie respected his mother, honoured her position as head of the Royal Family, and desperately needed maternal love and affection. Victoria, for her part, hated to think that her position was threatened in any way, and loathed the idea of giving Bertie power because, in a sense, this acknowledged that one day she would die and relinquish her authority altogether. And temperamentally she was incapable of loving Bertie well. She could feel close – well, fairly close – to her first-born daughter, Vicky. But a son, her heir, almost her rival, was too much of a challenge. To give room in her heart for Bertie would mean ousting Albert a fraction. And Albert demanded 100 per cent devotion.

So great was Victoria's adoration of Albert that she made the biggest mistake possible in Bertie's upbringing. She declared that he should 'resemble his angelic dearest father in every respect, both in body and mind'. This is a mistake in any family; it was a tragedy in Bertie's case, for he bore no resemblance whatever to Albert in outlook, talents or character.

Albert was, by nature, a studious, hard-working type who enjoyed intellectual pursuits. He was a loner. He had no love of life. Bertie, on the other hand, revelled in life, despite the handicap of Saturn. For his rising sign was Sagittarius, the sign of the archer who fires endless arrows of endeavour for the sheer fun of doing so. Bertie loved 'having a go'. Once he got into his stride – and with Saturn on the Ascendant, there is often a slow, muddled development into manhood – he adored outdoor sports such as shooting, riding and hockey, and became quite good at indoor sports too, especially practical jokes, romping about at parties and, so it is said, bed-time frolics as well.

Bertie was a Sagittarian in outlook, and no mistake. Anyone with Sagittarius strong in his horoscope wants to see what's happening on the other side of the horizon – by physical travel and by mental exploration, too. There is the predominantly outdoor type, which Bertie certainly was, and the egghead type, which he wasn't. He enjoyed wit, and he was excellent at the kind of far-ranging development of ideas to do with the destiny of nations. He was a diplomat, in short, rather than a professor, and far better suited to the craft of kingship than his father ever was. Yet Albert presumed, with the obsessive certainty of 'a man of reason', to lay down a rigid curriculum of study, discipline and moral improvement. It was called 'The Plan', and nothing was allowed to frustrate its working.

Young Bertie was subjected to a régime of book-study and harsh physical exercise, six days a week. He met no other children, except his own brothers and sisters occasionally, and spent his entire time in the company of adults, all of whom were intent on moulding him to a particular pattern. In his horoscope there is an exact Mercury–Saturn semi-sextile aspect which means a somewhat backward academic development and an inferiority complex as far as schooling is concerned. This Bertie certainly had. But the more he failed, the harsher became the régime as the Prince Consort redoubled his efforts to din some sense into the boy.

Victoria and Albert should have agreed to Bertie's own wishes, for they correspond exactly with the indications in his birth-chart. With the two 'masculine' planets, Saturn and Mars, close to the eastern horizon, and with the Sun in the deep, intense sign of Scorpio, Bertie was well suited to a military life. He enjoyed male company, he liked weaponry, he responded excellently to orders that had a sensible purpose behind them, and with Sagittarius rising he was no snob. He could mix well, with the Sun in the Eleventh House.

But his parents were determined to give him a modern prince's education so that he would become some latterday Renaissance Man. It was all so silly.

The summer of 1861 marked the blossoming of Bertie's love life. At long last Prince Albert had allowed him to undergo some basic military training, and his fellow cadet officers smuggled an actress, Nellie Clifden, into barracks, where, with efficiency and gusto, she deflowered the nineteen-year-old heir to the throne. He stayed infatuated with her memory for a couple of years. But in the same summer he met his future wife, Princess Alexandra of Denmark, as part of a prearranged courtship ritual enabling the royal teenagers to see whether they liked the look of each other.

By direction – moving one planet a degree forward through the Zodiac for each year of life – the Moon had reached a conjunction with Venus, the planet of love, as sweet and genuinely loving an astrological aspect as could be found. But, as so often with Bertie, a sour note quickly intruded. His father found out about the Nellie liaison in November, just as he was contracting typhoid fever. Within a month, he was dead – and Victoria always maintained that it was the news of Bertie's escapade that killed beloved Albert.

Bertie was never forgiven. And this death of one parent and emotional severance of relations by the other is indicated by the fact that just as the Moon reaches Venus, it also opposes the dire planet Pluto. This Moon–Pluto opposition means 'a pulling-up of family roots' and 'deep emotional tension'.

Things brightened within a couple of years. Bertie married Alix in 1863, when Mercury (the symbol of marriage in his chart, because it rules the Seventh House) conjoined Jupiter, the ruler of his chart as a whole.

The popular image of Alexandra is a poignant one. She is pictured as a gentle, affectionate, almost innocent creature who was whisked away from a cheerful, if poor, family life in Copenhagen to become Bertie's neglected wife. She captured British hearts from the moment she stepped ashore at Dover to prepare for her wedding at Windsor, and her popularity has never diminished.

Astrology supports this picture of Alix – up to a point. She was born on 1 December 1844, when the Sun was in Sagittarius and the Moon in Leo. These two Fire signs combine to give a warm, enthusiastic character. As you would expect with a Sagittarian girl, she was a tomboy in her childhood, and she never lost her enjoyment of larking about at country-house parties, whether this meant squirting soda-syphons at guests or practical jokes in the bedrooms. Like nearly all Sagittarians, she adored horses and dogs and was a very sporty lady, delighting particularly in skating which she accomplished, even with her chronic lame leg.

The problem with Alix is that we do not know her time of birth. This raises the fascinating subject of speculative astrology, which tries to guess her correct birth-time by seeing which horoscope, for various times of the day in question, suits her character best.

What we have, to start with, are simply the planetary positions in the Zodiac. We do not know how to orientate this map to the horizon. We have no Ascendant or Midheaven, nor do we know in which Houses the planets lie. So we must discover what is missing from her incomplete horoscope and then supply it by means of House-positions of planets.

This is a long process, and the end results are, at best, inspired guesswork. But one or two examples, in the case of Queen Alexandra, will show how the system works.

Let's start with the Ascendant, giving Alix's outer temperament. What were the qualities that people first noticed about her? Well, she was frank and lively, but Sagittarius accounts for that. She was considerate of others, which might suggest Libra rising, but she could also be quick-tempered, which does not sound like gentle Libra. Hang on a minute, though. The planet Mars, representing warmth, energy and anger, too, lay in Libra on Alix's birthday. Suppose that the early degrees of Libra were rising above the eastern horizon at the moment of birth. That would put Mars still just below the horizon, in the all-important First House, making her agreeable and polite, thanks to Libra, *and* bustling and hot-tempered, owing to Mars. What's more, it would put Pluto, the planet of doom and gloom, in the Seventh House, dealing with her marriage. There's no doubt that this relationship was fraught with problems after the blissful first few years.

The trouble with this plausible little hypothesis is that it fails to account for Alix's notorious unpunctuality and sleepiness. Often she did not rise from bed until eleven in the morning. She dithered around her boudoir, and she made no effort whatever to mend her ways. 'Keep him waiting; it will do him good!' she said of her husband, and kept waiting he was, hour upon hour at times. Now this trait was not simply the result of a half-awake disposition; there was an element of independent obstinacy as well. And this prompts me to guess that Alix had Aquarius as her Ascendant.

She looks Aquarian – tall and slim, narrow head, well-marked eyebrows and the tell-tale curl of the eyelid giving a slight lazy droop. And she behaved as an Aquarian – totally classless in her outlook, often putting the welfare of her servants before her own convenience, honest to the point of tactlessness, and, at times, stubborn, particularly when she became Queen. No one could remember what a queen should wear at a coronation. 'I know better than all the milliners and antiquaries,' she wrote. 'I shall wear exactly what I like.'

If the middle of Aquarius is 'chosen' as her putative Ascendant, she would have Neptune rising. Neptune in this position gives a person a fey, slightly dreamy demeanour together with a poor grasp of day-to-day reality. It would be the complete opposite of Edward's Saturn. He loved ceremonial pomp, niceties of etiquette and punctuality. She was much more lackadaisical.

In addition, she would have the Moon in her Seventh House in Leo, just like our present Queen. This bestows on the individual the ability to be charming and affable towards others – not in a false style but as part of a natural considerateness.

Alexandra is sometimes painted as a pure woman to whom sex was relatively unimportant. To the extent that this is true, Aquarius rising accounts for it, for anyone with Aquarius strongly positioned in their chart looks for companionship and mental rapport first, with physical passion running a close second. But in Alexandra's case, the two sexy planets, Venus and Mars, are absolutely side by side, so she undoubtedly had a powerfully flowing libido. The tragedy of her marriage is echoed in a sharp little configuration in her horoscope. For Saturn, the planet which causes disappointments and deprivations, forms an awkward, hurtful square aspect to Mars and Venus. This indicates sexual loneliness and heartache. In itself, it could also indicate a jealous, vindictive nature – but, thanks to her Sagittarian Sun and, probably, Aquarian Ascendant, Bertie's wife was incapable of being nasty to her husband. 'Jealousy', she wrote to a relative, 'is the bottom of all mischief and misfortune in this world.'

There was plenty to be jealous about. After the first few years of marriage, when Alexandra's increasing deafness made normal conversation very trying, Bertie started looking elsewhere. To some extent, this emotionally immature man was led astray by the bucks and young bloods, known as the Marlborough House set, which so distressed his mother the Queen. Bertie was certainly a highly sexed man, for he had, after all, the lusty planet Mars placed in the goaty sign of Capricorn – as good an indication of Pan-like appetites as you can find in astrology – and this was squared by Venus on one side and Pluto on the other. His lust, in other words, was like the umpire at a tennis match – caught between the sweet affection of Venus-in-Libra and the deep, instinctive urges of Pluto-in-Aries. The blessing of this arrangement is that he could happily roll off to Paris and hob-nob with *demi-monde* courtesans and, quite without hypocrisy, gladly return to a loving family life at Sandringham. But, like a true Sagittarian-rising individual, he could never settle for one or the other. He had to have both.

The truth is that Edward's sexual imbroglios were greatly exaggerated by a scandal-hungry Press. There is something deliciously intriguing about a portly, dignified pillar of society leading a juicy after-hours existence at music halls and private dining rooms and artists' studios and decadent *salons*.

Edward began his *boulevardier* life in the mid-1860s, just when Venus had moved by direction to form a conjunction with his Sun in the Eleventh House. This marked the start of his 'career', which is meant as an irony but also as a serious statement of fact. Edward's friendships were catholic, especially in comparison with Victoria's small court coterie. He mixed with Jews, freemasons, brash new plutocrats from both sides of the Atlantic, traditional aristocracy and a wide section of the nineteenth-century middle classes. Most important of all, thanks to the proliferating marriage links of Victoria's progeny, he was 'Uncle of Europe'. On many occasions he was able to affect foreign relations by a judicious letter to a nephew or brother-in-law or a word in so-and-so's ear when next they met at Cannes or Baden-Baden. The *Entente Cordiale*, which Edward as King forged with France, is an apt epitaph for a kindly man of great *bonhomie* who was a popular monarch after the living death of Victoria's final years.

Not that Edward was always loved by the public at large. Every so often, in most people's lives, there comes a year when everything goes badly – in career, in love, in health, in fortune generally. Astrology can nearly always spot these years in advance. In Edward's case, the planet responsible was old Saturn which occupied such an important position in his horoscope from the start.

Saturn moves round the Zodiac about once every thirty years. For someone like Edward, with Saturn so prominent in horoscope and personality, the thirtieth year was bound to be a difficult time. Sure enough, 1871 was a disaster for the Prince. He was exposed to scandal for the first time when a Lady Mordaunt, being sued for divorce by her husband, confessed that she had 'done wrong' with 'the Prince of Wales and others, often and in open day'. This hint of adultery coincided with a fierce wave of republicanism that could have toppled the Throne. 'The Queen is invisible and the Prince of Wales is not respected', noted Gladstone, and, horror of horrors, Bertie was booed as he arrived at Ascot. He was imperturbable, of course, and after his horses, quoted as favourites, won their races, he shouted back at the crowd: 'You seem in a better temper now . . . damn you!'

Worst of all, in 1871, was his attack of typhoid fever. By December, the doctors were giving up hope, and on the 14th, the anniversary of dear Albert's demise, the end seemed near. Victoria need not have worried. Her son survived, thanks to a wonderfully beneficial Jupiter transit on that day, to become a hugely popular public figure once again.

The next time Saturn struck, this time in his sixtieth year, was when he ascended the throne in 1901. This shows the positive side of Saturn, which is concerned with responsibility and hard work as much as disappointment and pain.

Victoria's son survived fever to become King. Edward's did not. Prince Albert Victor Christian Edward, generally known as Eddie, was born, two months early, at nine o'clock in the evening of

8 January 1864, after Bertie and Alix had spent the day ice-skating. As their first-born, he was Alix's favourite, but he was a disappointment to both of them – indeed, to the whole Royal Family. Despite a careful and fairly sympathetic upbringing, he simply did not seem to be the right material from which to fashion a future King. He was slow, backward, constantly in the shadow of his more clever younger brother Georgie, and morally lax. He would not persevere. He was dreamy, dull. They tried everything – private tutors, a time at Cambridge, a post as subaltern in the 10th Hussars – but nothing seemed to wake him up. All he wanted to do was enjoy himself, but he was not quite robust enough for a life of dissipation, even in his twenties. His delicate, poetic good looks started to look hollow.

They drew up a list of possible brides. He made advances towards Alix of Hesse, but she rejected him. Then he declared himself in love with Princess Hélène d'Orleans, the attractive daughter of the Comte de Paris who had one fatal drawback; she was a Roman Catholic, and no heir to the throne, by law, was allowed to marry a Catholic. Well, there was Princess May, a quiet and pleasant girl from the Royal House of Denmark. As soon as the name was mentioned, Eddie fell in love with her. Within days he had proposed. Everyone was delighted.

A month later, in January 1892, he contracted pneumonia and died. His parents were heartbroken. 'I have buried my angel today,' she wrote on the day of his funeral, 'and with him my happiness.' 'Gladly would I have given my life for his,' wrote Bertie. Sure enough, Saturn that month was directly conjunct his Moon ('sadness in the family') while on the day of his death Mercury was exactly conjunct Saturn ('mental depression').

What kind of a king would Albert Victor have been, had he lived? Would his dissipated lifestyle have been tolerated by the British public? My own view is that Eddie would have changed once he was thirty years old. He was a very Earthy soul, with Virgo rising and the Sun and Moon both in Capricorn. You might think this would make him a highly organized person with a firm grip on reality, but Capricorn folk are often slow beginners and, what's more, the Sun and Moon also lay in the Fifth House, devoted to pleasures and enjoyment. Eddie simply needed time – time to develop self-confidence, time to burst out of the suffocating blanket of failure that had surrounded him from birth. Like all Capricornians, he needed security, and the right marriage would have made the world of difference to him.

As it was, Georgie – who always beat him at everything – got his wife as well as his crown.

Georgie and May

The dandy and wit Max Beerbohm once wrote some verses describing the deadening court life revolving around George V and Queen Mary. A fictitious lady-in-waiting is heard wailing in Windsor Castle:

'Slow pass the hours, ah, passing slow;
My doom is worse than anything
Conceived by Edgar Allan Poe:
The Queen is duller than the King.'

To which an equally fictitious lord-in-waiting replies:

'Lady, your mind is wandering,
You babble what you do not mean;
Remember, to your heartening,
The King is duller than the Queen.'

Beerbohm was being dreadfully unfair, because the kind of monarchy he would have preferred – something elegant, vivacious and ever so slightly decadent – would not have kept the British Throne secure for more than five minutes, and not, certainly, in the troubled times of George's reign from 1910 to 1936. Yet I can't help concurring with Max. However worthy and estimable this royal couple may have been, they remain a pretty dull pair.

The Royal Family during the last hundred years shows a picture of various individuals struggling to cope with the demands that their position placed upon them. For none of them was it easy, for often it meant suppressing their real feelings and talents for much of the time. It involved being two people, a public *persona* and a private personality, which implies that every royal individual

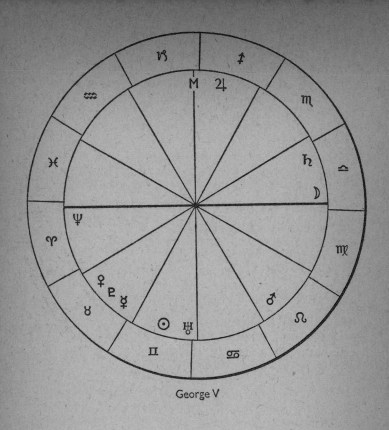

George V

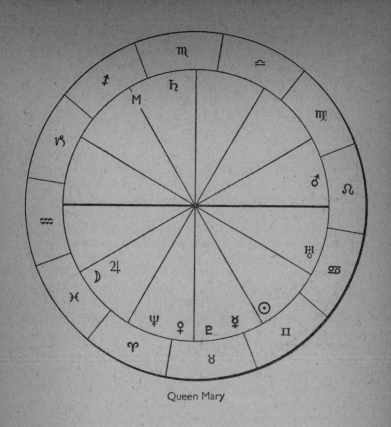

Queen Mary

is, by training, a bit of a schizoid – six of this, half a dozen of that – without connecting the two halves of the personality.

It is deeply interesting to me that the two monarchs who have coped most successfully with this dilemma are the Geminians, Queen Victoria and George V. Neither of them really expected to ascend to the throne, but both adapted themselves admirably to the demands of their calling. It must be the dual nature of Gemini, whose symbol is the mirror likeness of the twins, which explains this phenomenon.

Geminians are boyish all their lives. Their childhood experiences leave a deep impression on their psyches, and, just as Adam and Eve were loath to leave Eden, so are Geminians unwilling to depart from the thrilling innocence of their tender years. This applies more to Geminian boys than girls – possibly because instinctively we expect men to be more 'mature' than women. The transition from boyhood to manhood, in other words, tends to be sharp and divisive, while women, whatever their age, are appreciated more if they remain girlish. Certainly this has been true until the rise of the modern Ms. But, of all the signs, Gemini finds it hardest to bridge that gap between boy and man. The Geminian male, by some means or other, wants to remain the eternal adolescent.

George V may have been the bluff old sailor-king to his millions of subjects throughout the Empire, but from the moment he was born, on 3 June 1865, at half-past-one in the morning, he was little Georgie to his family. In return, his mother Alix was Motherdear, and was called by this mawkish name until her death sixty years later. There is a special astrological reason for this close link between mother and son. You will remember that the Moon, symbolizing the Mother, was in the Tenth House (to do with career) in Edward VII's chart, so that Queen Victoria was as much a superior at work as a simple straightforward mother to young Bertie. In Georgie's chart, the Moon occupies a very important position on the edge of the western horizon, just on the cusp of the Seventh House. This Seventh House is concerned with other people in general and the marriage partner especially, so in Georgie's case the beloved Motherdear was a wife as much as an adoring mum. Don't misunderstand me; there is no suspicion of incest between these royal paragons of virtue! But there was an extraordinarily close intimacy of feeling quite untypical of the Victorian Age in which they lived. Like Peter Pan (a great Geminian archetype) Georgie was never allowed to grow up. Even when he was nineteen years old, Motherdear was hoping that 'I shall always find my little Georgie quite the same and unchanged in every respect' – and her son, happy to be Peter Pan, would write as a grown man about 'that sweet little room of mine' at Sandringham and how 'you must go and see it sometimes and imagine that your Georgie dear is living in it.' Both of them had cracking tempers at times but George remained patient and loving towards his mother, while she, even in her eighties, described herself as 'your poor old blind and deaf old loving Motherdear.'

Georgie remained this mixture of tenderness and grumpiness all his life. His fiery nature came from his Ascendant, which was the sign of Aries. The sweetness and light emanated from his Moon in the opposite sign of Libra. His outer temperament was volatile, and he could fly off the handle if things were not to his liking. He had the direct, no-nonsense approach of the Ariean as well as the love of outdoor activities associated with this sign. He enjoyed hunting and shooting, and 'my most favourite place in all the world' was the country estate that his father created, Sandringham in Norfolk. Nearly all his childhood was spent at this house, and as soon as he married he took his bride to their permanent home, York Cottage, which stood within the Sandringham purlieus. It was a wretched little residence, far too small and close to mother-in-law for the bride's comfort, and already furnished by Georgie and a 'man from Maple's' in solid middle-class tastelessness. Georgie was quite insensitive to her wishes. He couldn't understand why his new wife, Princess May, wasn't head over heels in love with the place. People with Aries rising have these blind spots. They are so certain that their outlook is the commonsensical one that it never occurs to them that anyone else should have a contrary opinion.

Yet he was a doting husband. Theirs was a strange courtship, for of course May was initially engaged to the elder brother, Eddie. She was born on 26 May 1867, just before midnight, which made her a Geminian like Georgie, but with Aquarius rising. There are, in fact, a great number of similarities between their charts, for not only were their Suns in the same sign but both had Mercury, Venus and Pluto in the adjoining sign of Taurus, and in both cases the planet Mars lay in Leo. These links explain partly why King George and Queen Mary made such a successful royal marriage. They were both adaptable, both capable of responding to events and changing their characters to suit the prevailing circumstances. Yet in significant ways they were somewhat incompatible.

The difference of Ascendants explains a lot. Georgie, as we have seen, had Aries rising. It made him a man who respected facts, with a downright, practical streak in his nature. May, on the other hand, was all Air, with Aquarius rising and another Air sign, Gemini, as her Sun-sign. She was interested in ideas. She was constantly trying to improve her mind. She attended theatres and concerts for her own pleasure, and toured hundreds of exhibitions out of public duty, and wherever she went her mind was busy, inquisitive, learning all the time. She turned herself into an expert in antiques, especially her favourite period of the late eighteenth century. She did not take things for granted. Georgie, however, prided himself on not reading books, which is one reason why the philistine middle classes took him to their heart.

The other great difference was the fact that Georgie had the planet Jupiter nearest his Midheaven, while for May the planet closest to due south was Saturn. With Jupiter so prominent, King George was a lucky man as far as his career was concerned. He had a great sense of fair play, and in an age of rebellion and open class conflict he managed, thanks to the benign influence of Jupiter, to occupy the middle ground in the mind of the British public. He was a deeply conservative man, true enough, but he conveyed the impression that he was King of all the peoples, high or low, pink or brown; and in his dealings with the Labour governments of the inter-war years he established, better than his father ever could have done, that the British monarchy could play a quietly discreet, necessary role within a modern democracy. Above all, despite his testiness at times, George was a genial man, fond of chaff and banter, at home in the naval officer's mess. Nobody with Jupiter on the Midheaven could be an extremist, and George V's great role in a turbulent age was to hold the monarchy steady.

Queen Mary helped him enormously, in her own way. She could not be as warm as her husband, due to the presence of Saturn, poised like an iron hand controlling her personality. She was a woman of indomitable will-power, though she never exercised this power in a personally ambitious way. Hers was a moral strength, a conception of royal duty that kept easy-going George on the straight and narrow. When she married him, in 1893, court circles were apprehensive about Prince George, now second in line to the throne. He was likeable but rather schoolboyish: a typically immature Geminian, in fact. Lord Esher, indeed, described him as the *garçon eternel*. With resolution and tact, his young wife helped to mould him into the future King. Her famous Saturn was directly opposite the ruler of his chart, Mercury, and at times she must have been disappointed by his lack of intellectual distinction. May was no bluestocking, but at least she *tried*. Georgie blithely retained his contempt for the world of ideas.

This is one of the oddities of his horoscope. Geminians, especially someone like George with his Sun in the communicative Third House, tend to be facile thinkers and writers. If he had not been born into the Royal Family, he could have been a good salesman, lecturer or teacher. Yet his writings are as unstylish as a naval log-book, with none of the urbane élan that his father King Edward could muster in the choice of words and phrases. Queen Mary, too, although a Geminian herself, suffered from paroxysms of shyness whenever she was required to speak in public. The BBC possesses only one recording of her voice – a couple of sentences when she was launching a ship. And yet her chart, with the Sun on the cusp of the theatrical Fifth House and the Moon in conjunction with Jupiter, is the horoscope of a born actress.

I have no doubt that George and Mary were made dull by the roles they were forced to carry out in the service of the British people. Geminians have difficulty in growing up; and one short cut to maturity, so they think, is to maintain the values and customs of their childhood. They fight against their own nature by wearing the false colours of the conservative, just as the trees which sway most gracefully with the wind need the deepest roots

65

if they are to survive. George was absurdly traditional, wearing the same design of gloves throughout life that were in fashion when he was a boy and always creasing his trousers on the sides, never down the fronts, because that was the midshipman's regulation dress when he first joined the Royal Navy as a teenager.

Queen Mary, in turn, was a rigorous upholder of the *done thing*. She lived her life by clockwork, always rising at 7.15, always in her boudoir by 9.30, always embroidering in the hour before lunch, always making a little trip to an art gallery or exhibition in the afternoon, always retiring for the night at 10.45. As her widowhood advanced into the 1940s and 1950s, the British public saw her as the sole surviving link with the *ancien régime*. Poor May! a young-old figure all her life, youthful in her interests and sharp grasp of daily routine, aged in her stultified values. She reigned as Queen Consort during the pinnacle and decline of the British Empire, but could not change her ways as rapidly as the world itself.

She was a rock past which the twentieth-century current raced – a rock, indeed, against which her brilliant, wayward son David stumbled to his doom.

David and Wallis

By popular reckoning the Royal Family is divided into goodies and baddies. In each generation, it seems, one individual is acclaimed as the paradigm of royal virtue, while a near-relative, often a brother or sister, is portrayed as . . . well, not quite measuring up to the job. Queen Victoria herself, the founder of the modern Royal Family, assiduously tried to dissociate herself from her naughty, lax, boorish Hanoverian forbears; and ever since, whenever one of the Royals has departed from the acceptable code of conduct, public opinion has murmured: 'Well, it's the old Hanoverian blood asserting itself!'

Bertie in his Prince of Wales role was certainly considered to be letting the side down, though as King Edward he moved back into the goodies' camp. His elder son Eddie was clearly a baddie, though he, too, might have regained his virtue had he lived; in the event, the mantle of respectability passed to his younger brother Georgie, who could never be anything but a goodie.

Everyone assumed that the pattern could not be repeated in the next generation. In Edward Albert Christian George Andrew Patrick David, Prince of Wales and sprightly heir to the throne, the British monarchy had surely found a winner. No one suspected that this odds-on favourite would become an also-ran. The goodie turned virtually overnight into a baddie, and was never forgiven.

David, as he was known within the family circle, was born on 23 June 1894, at White Lodge, in Richmond Park, at ten o'clock in the evening. This makes him a Cancerian, and as his character unfolded it became evident that he was a true crab in many of his deeper aims and needs. But it is the Ascendant which shows early in anyone's personality and remains most clearly visible throughout

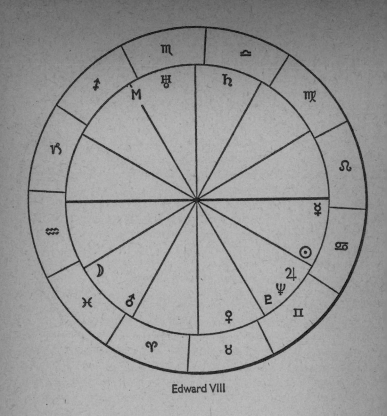

Edward VIII

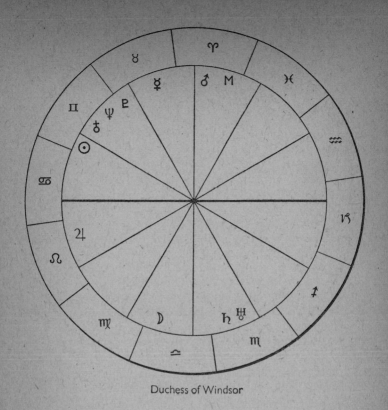

Duchess of Windsor

life, and in David's case this rising sign was Aquarius, the same as his mother's.

It is fascinating to see how two individuals, remarkably close in background and breeding, expressed the same rising sign in such diametrically opposed fashions. Mary, as we have seen, was a totally shy, undemonstrative woman. The sense of dispassion, which is a key feature of the Aquarian personality, manifested itself in total reserve, not only towards the public or courtiers but among her own family as well. She found it extremely hard, if not impossible, to express inner feelings, although there is no doubt, as her horoscope shows, that she was inwardly a lively, creative and basically optimistic soul.

David, on the other hand, was a natural mixer, though his extrovert qualities had to battle fiercely against an ingrained shyness as well. The ruler of Aquarius is the planet Uranus, and in Queen Mary's horoscope it is placed in the Sixth House, concerned with service to others. Her natural instinct was to put herself at the disposal of people, not out of charity but from a sense of duty. And she always knew where her duty lay. 'I have always to remember', she said about her children, 'that their father is also the King.' He came first; and just as the dutiful servant (or dog) follows no one but his own master, so Queen Mary was steadfast in her peculiarly stubborn Aquarian way to her liege lord, King George.

David's ruler, Uranus, stood high in the sky in the Tenth House, connected with career and public affairs. By temperament, therefore, he was well suited to a life on the public stage. He enjoyed playing the leader, assuming the role of managing director, taking firm grasp of the reins of power. He was born master, not servant.

Actually, this is only half-true. The tragedy of his life stemmed from a fundamental ambivalence within his birth-chart. In truth he was master *and* servant, for, whereas his ruler may have been lording it in the Midheaven, his Sun meekly resided in – yes, you've guessed it, the quiet, subdued Sixth House. By temperament, David may have been chairman of the company; by character, he was only the charlady.

From early childhood right through to the Abdication, David

had misgivings about the role he was required to play. He disliked the stuffy court regulations, and sought as Prince of Wales and as King Edward VIII to sweep away monarchical rigmarole that only got in the way of direct contact between the Royal Family and the British public. All this comes from Aquarius, the most 'democratic' of the Zodiac signs. We have seen similar behaviour in his grandmother, Queen Alexandra, who probably had Aquarius as her Ascendant, too. She liked children to be romping wild, while Queen Mary, a much more severe character, sought to give her children a rigorous, correct upbringing. All three of them – Alix, May and little David – were quite unsnobbish, which you would expect with their Aquarian Ascendants; but while Alix (through deafness) and May (through shyness) kept themselves to themselves, David actively wanted to become part of the crowd – a distinctive part, perhaps, but nonetheless 'One Of The People'.

Women played a vital role in David's life-story. Once again it's interesting to note how this interest in the opposite sex has ebbed and flowed from one royal generation to the next. Prince Albert and his grandson King George were the two abstemious males, and neither of them made love to anyone but his wife. Both of them, indeed, relished all-male company, Albert through his early contact with the Prussian officer class and Georgie through his early, fond experiences in the Royal Navy. King Edward, meanwhile, was a roisterous womanizer, and *his* grandson, the dashing Prince of Wales, actively enjoyed the company of women. Both of them, remember, had inadequate mothers who loathed pregnancy, birth and messy little babies; both of them were denied normal children as friends while they were growing up; and both of them had good astrological reasons for *needing* adorable women. In David's case, it was the fact that his Sun lay in Cancer.

Every Cancerian male passes through a number of distinct phases as he grows into maturity. (This growth pattern is broadly true of all men, of course, but is notably emphasized in those with Cancer strong in their charts.) The first phase, lasting until puberty, is unquestioning love between mother and child. The boy is said to be 'in thrall' with the mother archetype, according to Jungian psychologists, wrapped in her aura, feeding off her psychic energy.

The second phase coincides with the normal adolescent rebellion against parents, though in the Cancerian's case this revolt is a confused, sometimes half-hearted affair, for the boy is still deeply attached to his mother. The third phase, reached in adulthood, occurs when the Cancer man comes to terms with the mother archetype, acknowledging its existence but ready to be independent from it. The psychologists call this stage 'the constellation' of the archetype.

Now this process takes many different forms according to the circumstances of the boy concerned, and can be halted at any stage. It may not be focused on the physical mother at all, but on other people – or, for that matter, institutions – which become mother-figures in the boy's unconscious mind. Some Cancerians, for instance, never get beyond the first phase; throughout their lives, they remain fixated on Mother, dependent upon her, obeying her, constantly within her orbit. Other Cancerians reach the second stage of uneasy rebellion, fighting Mother but still not out of her grasp. Best of all, if it can be achieved, is the third phase when the Cancerian male, in a sense, becomes Mother himself; he recognizes that there is something of an old woman about him, that he fusses too much, that he loves making people feel at home, that – at a higher level – he needs to act in a caring, cherishing, nurturing way towards his 'children' who may be real people, or works of art, or plants in his garden, or anything he takes under the comfort of his wing.

This natural process is bound to be disturbed whenever the women in the boy's earliest days fail to fulfil their role as Mother. We have already seen that Queen Mary was a stiff, awkward woman as far as close personal relations were concerned. She couldn't cope with her first child, David: 'I really believe he begins to like me at last,' she wrote to his father, 'he is most civil to me.' Cancerian boys do not want to be 'civil'. They want to bury their faces in the soft, beloved breast.

David claimed later to have had no love in his childhood. His first nurse was a sadistic, incompetent woman who would pinch him just before he was taken to see his parents. Naturally he bawled his head off, and was hastily returned to the ever-loving care of the nurse. His mother was cold and strict, just as Queen Victoria had been with Bertie; and, appropriately enough, just as Bertie had a cold Moon–Saturn aspect in his birth-chart, so did David in his.

He suffered equally bad relations with his father. 'I was always frightened of my father', King George was reported to say, adding about his own children, 'they must be frightened of me.' Not only was David a very different character to his father; there was deep animosity between them. George's Mars, representing his anger, was directly opposite David's Ascendant, while, in turn, Mars in David's chart was very close to his father's own Ascendant. In consequence, they were daggers drawn towards each other, David despising his father's taciturn conservatism and George anxious and nonplussed by his son's extraordinary and (to his eyes) outrageous behaviour at times. He surrounded David with a wall of cautionary *don'ts*. Don't go steeplechasing, don't drive such fast cars, don't fly your own aeroplane, don't dress in such bright, ungentlemanly clothes. A wise father can tactfully help to wean the Cancerian boy from the maternal archetype. Gruff, bluff old King George had no idea that the problem even existed.

So David grew up, a superficially bright but not clever young man, lonely, nervously taut, full of wiry vitality that made him love outdoor sports and hate bookish activities. As he blossomed from naval cadet to Oxford undergraduate to Prince of Wales, he became more confident. His disarming smile captured public attention all over the world. At this time, in the 1920s, radio and newsreels and popular newspapers vied with each other to boost circulation, and with the rise of Hollywood came the Star System, in which people became Personalities overnight. The Royal Family, aided by scrupulous court advisers, had always maintained a respectful distance between the Monarch and the People. But the young Prince of Wales, eager to be treated as 'One of Us', was bewitched by the modern media. Away from court etiquette on his famous solo world tours, he laughed, danced, shook hands, gave interviews, paid visits, slept little and exuded such energy that the Press could hardly keep up with him.

He became, of course, the most eligible bachelor in the world, as the popular song *I Danced With the Man Who Danced With the Girl Who Danced With the Prince of Wales* testified. But, however many girls surrounded him, there was only one kind with whom he seemed to associate on anything like a long-term basis: not young girls, but married women such as Freda Ward and Thelma Furness.

He met Mrs Ward in the spring of 1918, and for the next fifteen years conducted his love affair with her in complete discretion. Every day he was in London, usually at five in the afternoon, he would arrive at her house and spend the evening there. If he had an evening dinner engagement, he would return afterwards as soon as possible. They spent days together at country houses of friends, and weeks together at her Normandy hideaway. Their liaison was well-known within London society, but never mentioned in the newspapers.

When they first met, his Venus (planet of love) conjoined Jupiter (planet of happiness) while the Moon had moved by direction to a conjunction with Mars. There is no doubt that he was passionately in love with her – indeed, at one stage proposed marriage, which Mrs Ward carefully and wisely turned down. His other, more publicized, affair with Lady Furness was basically a physical relationship, but with Freda there were deeper links. But why married women? Why not eligible girls fit to be Queen of England?

One reason is the basic ambiguity of his outlook, half-master and half-servant. He *worshipped* the women in his life in an abject, almost masochistic way. Astrologically the explanation for this is the fact that Neptune (the planet most closely associated with masochism) was half-way between the Sun and Venus when he was born. The way in which he sought to express love (Sun–Venus) was a Neptunian way: limp, tender, highly idealistic, greatly susceptible, with him playing the soft-voiced adorer and the woman a more vital and authoritarian role. In short, he wanted to be mothered.

A second reason, supported by rumour but not by astrology, is that he was quasi-homosexual anyway, with his love of embroidery (taught by his mother), his interest in dressing up in women's clothes at times, and the way his voice would go shrill when he was excited. There is no evidence in his birth-chart, apart from the general observation that he was a mother's boy, that the Prince was bisexual or that he sought to hide any incipient homosexuality by resorting with older, more experienced women.

A third reason, much better founded in astrological evidence, is that David never wanted to marry a woman who would be accepted by the Establishment. With Aquarius strong, he hated the idea of getting something for nothing – of inheriting power and position simply through the accident of birth. He wanted the monarchy on his terms, and the *only* means at his disposal was to choose as wife a woman that nobody else would find acceptable.

If this sounds far-fetched, bear in mind that his Midheaven (i.e. his career as King) neatly bisects the arc between Venus and Neptune. If Venus and Neptune together mean 'romantic idealism and unreality', then it follows that the Prince was obsessed with the need to link his inner love with his outer duty. Did he not say in his abdication broadcast: 'I have found it impossible to carry the heavy burden of responsibility and to discharge my duties as King as I would wish to do without the help and support of the woman I love.' And no one can doubt that his attachment to Mrs Wallis Simpson was a highly Venus–Neptune relationship: unreal, out of this world, more than a little fantastic.

It began in the early 1930s, first as a purely social contact and by the spring of 1934, when the Prince was nearing the dangerous age of forty, as a more intimate and demanding friendship. At this time Wallis Simpson was living in London with her second husband. She had been born two years after the Prince, in 1896, in the same month, June, but on the 19th, making her a Geminian instead of a Cancerian, at seven o'clock in the morning, to a slightly down-at-heel Baltimore couple. Her father died when she was a few months old, and she was raised in decent penury by her mother and Uncle Sol, a banker and entrepreneur. She grew into a young lady who knew the value of money and was determined to make a success of life. She attained a reputation at school of being attractive to boys – 'rather fast', in fact – and at sixteen she was married to Earl Winfield Spencer, who turned out to be a neurotic alcoholic. After being locked in the bathroom by her drunken husband once too often, she obtained a divorce.

Soon after, Uncle Sol died and she discovered that she was left only a small trust fund that would cease anyway when she remarried. Wallis married a quiet, scholarly young lawyer called Ernest Simpson who was about to live in London. It was while they were still making friends in the capital that they were imperceptibly drawn into the Prince of Wales set.

Her character is resolutely Geminian: bright, vivacious, interested in trends and fashions, gay and flirtatious as a young woman and capable of preserving her youth well into old age. Just as David was the reverse side of the Aquarian coin compared with his mother the Queen, so was Wallis the reverse of Gemini. I have a theory that one reason why Queen Mary was so implacably opposed to David's proposed marriage to Wallis was that in this American divorcee the dour English Queen could see everything she herself *might have been*, but for the grace of God . . .

The outer temperament of Wallis, shown by her Ascendant, is Cancer, and this is the strong link with her future husband David. She was capable of playing Mother, for she was careful, considerate, sympathetic and nicely bossy. 'She forbade the Prince to smoke during the *entr'acte* in the theatre itself', noted Harold Nicolson in the early days of her association with David. 'She is clearly out to help him.' Clearly, too, David was out to impress her. Within weeks, polite society in London was scandalized by the way in which the couple seemed to flaunt themselves. He gave her 100,000 pounds' worth of jewellery in their first year together, and she was described 'literally smothered in rubies'. The Prince was in love, and astrology bears this out. In his fortieth year, his planet of love, Venus, had moved by direction to form a conjunction with the Sun, so this really was the miraculous year for a blossoming of his love. The trouble, in his case, was that Venus was totally unaspected in his birth-chart, so that no other planet formed a strong link with it. His love nature, in other words, was curiously dissociated from the remainder of his personality, and he found it hard to integrate it. It tended to behave of its own accord, and when highly stimulated, as it was in 1934, it seemed to lose all sense of propriety. During the next year, when Mars had moved in direct opposition to Uranus, he must have been under strong manic pressure to break the rules.

This planetary aspect induces a rebellious streak, with more than a hint of danger involved. Two events followed from this. The Prince's sex life must have been much more lively and boisterous than usual, suggesting that Wallis, unlike her predecessors, was able to calm him down and cure him of his habitual nervousness. And the old King died, plunging David into the loneliest job in the world.

This Mars–Uranus opposition spilled over into 1936, the one and only year of King Edward VIII's reign. From the start, while his father's body was still warm, he ordered all the clocks at Sandringham to be turned back to Greenwich Mean Time (as a quirk of Edward VII they had been half-an-hour fast for donkey's years). This act of near-hysteria, which deeply shocked his family and servants, pervaded many of his actions at this time. He seemed totally absorbed in his personal crisis, and treated his staff with no consideration and tackled his kingly duties with no persistence whatever. The famous red boxes sent daily from the Foreign Office were neglected for many weeks, down at his private hideaway, Fort Belvedere, and official circles were so worried about the King's state of mind and his association with Wallis Simpson that Special Branch officers followed him – and her – everywhere, in case of a breach of security.

If the Mars–Uranus opposition made the King burn with indignation, several other astrological factors were at work to mark 1936 as his year of crisis. By transit, the planet Pluto formed a close conjunction all year with his Mercury. This corresponds with acute mental obsession verging on paranoia. Through his own volition he was breaking friendships, clanging the iron door of silence in the face not only of his personal companions but the Establishment in general. Only one person mattered; only she could be trusted; only she would give wise advice; and, to the horror of Court and Cabinet, Parliament and public, Mrs Simpson became the single dominant force in his life.

The Abdication Crisis is too well-known to be recounted, and, in a sense, is quite extraneous to the real battle within David's heart. To him there was no constitutional dilemma. It was a straightforward determination that *his* woman should be Queen of England, and, as the Labour politician J. H. Thomas put it to

Harold Nicolson at the time: "Ere we 'ave this obstinate little man with 'is Mrs Simpson. Hit won't do, 'arold. I tell you that straight.'

The British Establishment, led by Queen Mary and the Archbishop of Canterbury, agreed. It just would not do.

The Abdication itself was comparatively easy for the King, because he did not want to be monarch – not on *their* terms. With Uranus in the Tenth House, he could have been a brilliant ruler, an erratic one, a modern one, but he could never have been a dull constitutional ruler. He could have served his country well, and for a time as Prince of Wales he captured more worldwide adulation than any other British monarch before or since. He was the Golden Boy, and he tarnished.

On 10 December 1936, when he yielded the Crown to his younger brother George, David heaved a sigh of relief. Mercury and Jupiter together, meaning travel, contacted his Sun, and he slipped across the Channel to exile on the Continent. Equally appropriate, Neptune was exactly square to Jupiter in his chart, triggering off the conjunction that these planets form at birth. The interpretation of this aspect is 'the well-meaning fool' and 'living in a fool's paradise'. He was a kind, sensitive man who craved home and family; and, because he was denied true family happiness as a child, he exiled himself with a woman who, he felt, could provide the long-awaited boon of motherliness. Yet they had no children. He had his home, his beloved garden, his dogs. Otherwise they drifted, along with the well-to-do international set, from Paris to New York to Palm Springs to Cannes and back again. It was all such a waste.

In her chart the planet Saturn represents her marriage. It exactly conjoins his Uranus, signifier of his personality and career. In effect, their marriage became his career, his single *raison d'être*. He pined for her acceptance. He grew angry that *they* – the British Establishment – refused to acknowledge Wallis as Her Royal Highness. In exile the man who had spurned the trappings of privilege now clung to them more stubbornly than ever.

That boyish, melancholy face will haunt the pages of British history. It was his personal tragedy that he could not constellate his Cancerian archetype and come to terms with his own nature. It was the tragedy of the Royal Family that they could not provide the proper fertile family soil in which he could put down his roots.

George and Elizabeth

For the second time in less than fifty years the British Crown
passed from elder to younger brother – once through abrupt and
premature death, once through dereliction of duty. Eddie and
David had both been groomed for office from their earliest days,
but George V and George VI, as younger sons, had expected a
fairly quiet, well-ordered life in the Royal Second XI. It was a
momentous surprise to both of them to be suddenly appointed
school captain.

At least, in George V's case, he had been recognizably the
brighter and more able of the brothers. His own son, Prince
Albert, later the Duke of York and King George VI, was
demonstrably slower and more introvert than his gay, charming
sibling David. Whereas David enjoyed publicity, Bertie shunned
the limelight. David had the happy knack of saying the right thing
to the right person, be he an American radio reporter or a South
Wales unemployed miner. Bertie stammered horribly, and always
felt gauche and hesitant in public. Yet the verdict of history is
plain: whatever the reasons, whatever the excuses, David's life
was a failure and Bertie's a success. David began with high
promise and moved inexorably towards lonely and embittered
exile. Bertie, through deep reserves of character, rose to the
occasion and triumphed.

It was a triumph of modesty.

Bertie's upbringing was identical to David's – narrow,
disciplined, lacking warm parental attention – but he seemed to
survive the ordeal much better. He was equally sensitive and
nervous, but became a more balanced adult than his highly-strung
elder brother. Why was this?

When Bertie was born (14 December 1895, Sandringham, about
3.05 a.m.) the sign of Libra was rising above the eastern horizon.

With this Libran Ascendant, it was natural for him to aim towards balance and harmony all his life, for the symbol of Libra is the pair of scales. Any Libra-rising individual has a built-in gentleness of manner. He does not want to rock the boat or stir up mischief. His own desire is to maintain peace and equilibrium in his surroundings.

In Bertie's case, this quality was doubly emphasized by the presence of his ruler Venus just below the horizon, in the First House. You will recall that an earlier Prince Albert, his own great-grandfather, had a ruler in his First House – for him Mercury in Virgo, doubly emphasizing all the pernickety, clever, carping side of his nature. But Venus is all sweetness and light. Bertie was a naturally affectionate child and a truly loving father to his own children in later years. To his people, too, he exuded an air of caring. 'The quality of mercy is not strain'd', wrote Shakespeare, and the phrase aptly describes the sense of justice and fair play that George VI projected throughout the grim years of the Second World War.

Venus itself does not lie in Libra but the adjoining sign of Scorpio, which is a much tougher and more intense Zodiac influence. It's as though Bertie was born sweet (Libra) to become more determined (Scorpio) as his life proceeded. And there's another influence showing that his life would be an effortful one: the presence of Saturn in this First House side by side with Venus.

We have seen how Saturn in this position played a dominant part in the character of yet another Bertie, his grandfather Edward VII. Both men had a fine sense of duty, though both were thwarted in following the careers of their choice – old Bertie in the army and young Bertie in the Royal Navy. But there was a crucial difference. Edward VII, as a man of enormous gusto, was capable of expressing the gaudy, bawdy side of Saturn (for remember that the word derives from the Roman god who was celebrated in those great orgies of merriment, the Saturnalias; to good old Bertie, every day was a Saturday, a day to let off steam and relax). His grandson, George VI, saw the darker side of this coin: discipline, effort, physical pain and courage in the face of adversity.

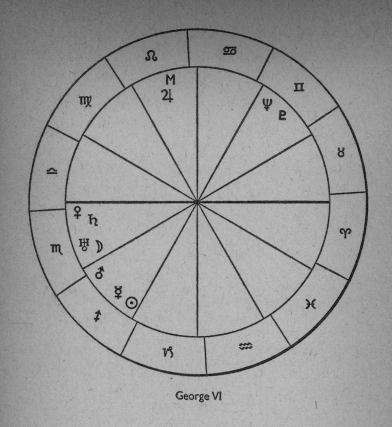

George VI

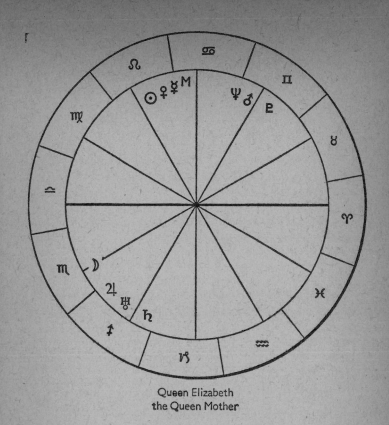

Queen Elizabeth
the Queen Mother

But it is a mistake to portray George VI simply as a quiet, sweet, helpless man who somehow held steady in the storm of war. Beneath his gentle exterior he was a true man of action, with Moon in Scorpio and Sun in the lively, adventurous sign of Sagittarius. His emotional disposition, in other words, was deep and searching, with a desire to get to grips with life and discover the truth underlying the facts. He took a precise, sometimes morbid interest in his own illnesses, for instance, and he paid more than lip-service to his religion. The Moon in Scorpio gives a marvellous capacity to keep secrets from others – and to keep faith with oneself and one's own high standards.

As a Sagittarian, he yearned for a life of physical excitement and adventure. He loved the out-of-doors, and could never abide office routine at his desk. This showed early, from the moment he entered the Royal Navy as a midshipman.

Until his adolescence, Bertie was as scared of his father as David was. But whereas David, from his teenage years on, needed to rebel against parental authority, Bertie assimilated himself within the prevailing family outlook and beliefs. This was not so much due to any lack of independence on Bertie's part – on the contrary, with the Sun in Sagittarius and the Moon side by side with the lively, unconventional Uranus, he was a man who needed to make up his own mind – but because Bertie and his father were quite alike and certainly shared many interests: principally a love of the Navy, but also quieter pursuits such as stamp-collecting and rural relaxations like huntin', shootin' and fishin'.

Both men's horoscopes were notably similar. The Ascendant–Sun combination, in each case, was Air or Fire, and their Moons were in Water signs. And whereas poor David's Mars was in direct contact with his father's fiery Ascendant, Bertie's Mars formed a more harmonious trine aspect. They both had Jupiter high in the southern sky – a sure sign of 'success at one's career' and indeed the old man's Jupiter was very close to young Bertie's Sun, signifying a genuine warmth and camaraderie between them. There was no doubt who was boss, with Father's Saturn slap-bang on top of his offspring's Ascendant; but it was a kindly parental influence, not a restricting one.

Perhaps the event which brought them closest together was the

First World War. David, as heir to the Throne, was cossetted and protected, much to his own annoyance; but Bertie was allowed, indeed encouraged, to see active service on the high seas. Much of his war was spoilt by the first sign of the gastric troubles that were to plague him all his life; they commenced at the moment that Saturn moved by direction to conjoin Mars, and produced a duodenal ulcer. But in his twentieth year, just when Mars moved to conjoin his Sun, he took part in the Battle of Jutland. He saw men die and ships sink, and he experienced direct gun-fire, some so close that, as he wrote to his father, 'I was distinctly startled and jumped down the hole in the top of the turret like a shot rabbit!' But he was not scared. He was filled with the glamour of Mars, the god of battle. 'It seems curious but all sense of danger and everything else goes except the one longing of dealing death in every possible way to the enemy.'

This planet Mars caused him much unhappiness in life, for with Libra rising his basic nature was quite antipathetic to its hot and hostile influence. Not only did it mark the weak link in his constitution, namely his digestive tract; it accounted for what Bertie called 'the curse that God has put upon me' – namely the stammer that afflicted him throughout life.

The two planets Mercury and Saturn symbolize 'the functional relationship of the nervous system with the organs of speech and hearing', according to the German astrologer Reinhold Ebertin in *The Combination of Stellar Influences*. Poor Bertie had the planet Mars poised exactly in between these bodies in his horoscope, so whenever he was angry or nervous he had great difficulty in co-ordinating his brain with his diaphragm. Hence the stutter. It was only through the help of a Harley Street specialist over many years, plus a tremendous effort of willpower, that Bertie managed to subdue his errant Mars. It's interesting to note that whenever he stammered badly, he was apt to lose his temper in frustration, for the energy of Mars, denied an outlook in speech, could only explode in anger.

It's fascinating, too, to note that the person who helped him most to overcome his speech defect was someone whose calm, benign Jupiter exactly conjoined his disruptive Mars: his sweet wife Elizabeth.

Queen Elizabeth, the Queen Mother, is the most gracious and respected member of the Royal Family alive, and I apologize for including her in the 'Past' section of this book. In a long life of public service, she has created no enemies, and this record of unblemished virtue could have been accurately foreseen in her horoscope at her moment of birth: 11.31 a.m. on 4 August 1900.

Like her future husband, she had the gentle, agreeable sign of Libra as her Ascendant. Like him, too, she had the Moon in Scorpio, so both of them had the inner strength to endure privation and yet maintain a sweet reasonableness on the surface. What gave Elizabeth the lovable warmth of her personality was the triple conjunction in Leo of three important celestial bodies: the Sun, Mercury and Venus, all in the Tenth House to do with her career. In effect, Elizabeth has made a career of her charm, for this conjunction has bestowed on her a sense of grace, of beauty and of soft good humour that has touched millions of people all over the world.

No wonder, therefore, that young Prince Albert, just created Duke of York, fell head over heels in love with the girl when they met at Glamis Castle in the autumn of 1921, for they had so much in common. But Elizabeth, like a true Libra-rising girl, took her time before deciding to accept his marriage proposal. It was a perfect time for each of them: he with the Moon moving serenely to form a conjunction with his Sun, she with an equally fruitful and apt trine aspect between these bodies in her birth-chart. They were married on 26 April 1923, amid general rejoicing.

Of all the royal couples in this book, George and Elizabeth are the best matched pair from an astrological point of view. Between them could flow a current of affection and understanding more easily than between any other marriage partners. All they wanted was a quiet family life with their young daughters Lilibet and Margaret Rose, he with his boys' clubs giving open-air holidays to deprived city children, she with her Girl Guides, each with their share of public duties but both thankfully returning to the peace of Royal Lodge, in Windsor Great Park, where they delighted in creating a small landscape garden of great beauty and taste.

Events moved them towards a greater destiny.

It was only in the autumn of 1936, a few months after his father's death, that the Duke of York realized that the new King's attachment to Mrs Simpson was deep, serious and obstinate. On 20 October he was told that Mrs Simpson was proceeding with her divorce, and that the Prime Minister thought that the possibility of abdication could no longer be avoided. The Duke hated the thought, so it is said, but astrologically it is clear that this was a moment of great opportunity, for Jupiter formed a transit with the Sun – exactly what you would expect for 'promotion at work'. At the same time, and for the next six weeks, Uranus was square to his Midheaven meaning 'a sudden turn of destiny' and 'a change of career'.

The crisis burst early in December. Within a week, no more, the British public had to adjust itself to the news that their debonair young King was abandoning his post forever, and that his place would be taken by his shy, withdrawn brother who seemed so incapable of putting two sentences together that people wondered whether he was all there in the head. He had received absolutely no training in statecraft; he had never seen any Foreign Office papers; and in those hungry 1930s, with unemployment rife and social revolution occurring throughout the world, how could this nonentity of a man have the vision to inspire his people?

He did it through sincerity, humility and a firm belief in God. His concept of monarchy was a king standing at the head of his people, sharing their dangers and hardships, identifying with their cause. He was the ideal ruler of the British people during the Second World War, for he was so self-evidently, like them, an amateur desperately battling against a brutish professional army. 'Thank God for a good King,' cried a man amid the rubble and ruins of bombed London, as George and Elizabeth moved without formality among them. 'Thank God for a good people,' answered the King, and a wave of mutual admiration swept between monarch and subjects.

The King never wavered in his certainty that the Allies would win. This was mainly due to the blessing of Jupiter on the Midheaven, which gives boundless optimism even in the face of danger. Elizabeth shared this positive approach, thanks to her own Jupiter–Midheaven trine. When Buckingham Palace was bombed, she declared: 'I'm so glad. It makes me feel I can look the East End in the face.'

If George VI personified one kind of Englishman – the reticent, stiff-upper-lipped gentleman determined to do his duty with a total absence of egotism – Winston Churchill harked back to an older, more vivid image: John Bull, the British bulldog, the Lion roaring in defiance. At first, George was opposed to Winston becoming Prime Minister. In his typically Libra-rising way, he hated to see hopeless Neville Chamberlain go. His first thought, as replacement, was the aristocratic, 'safe' Lord Halifax, but in the end the Labour Party forced him to send for Winston to form a Coalition Government.

They were made from the same mould, for both men had Libra as their Ascendant, both had Sun in Sagittarius. But whereas George had the planet Venus In the First House, rumbustious Winston had the two hot, tempestuous planets Mars and Jupiter there.

No nobler a Zodiacal combination than Libra and Sagittarius can be imagined. Together they provide valour coupled with justice, enterprise with good judgement. Winston, naturally, was the wilder of these two men; he revelled in argument, passion and his own magnetic personality, as you would expect with Mars and Jupiter so prominent. George lacked the pugnacious quality of Winston. He would have been a useless politician, dithering too long, unprepared to be devious or ruthless. But he was a fine constitutional monarch, and an admirable Supreme Commander during the war.

Down the centuries, supporters of royalty have asserted that monarchs rule by divine right. When the rise of democracy lessened the power of the Crown, they still maintained that an ineffable aura of divine goodness surrounded the royal figurehead. With yet further encroachments on the power and privilege of the Royal Family, it is hard to assert that the 'magic' of our Head of State is anything more than hopeful public relations.

But in those grim days of war, George and Winston were the heroes of Britain. Who knows what spiritual power was channelled through them to be radiated to the peoples of the Allied cause? For George, apparently helpless, proved a victor in the end, just as Jupiter on the Midheaven promised that he always would.

Part Two **Present**

Elizabeth and Philip

In retrospect, it is easy to see that each generation gets the royalty that it deserves – or rather, the royalty that is appropriate for the times. No one can doubt that Victoria embodied many of the virtues – and defects – of the Age that bears her name. Edward VII was exactly the right monarch for that last great flourish of the leisured past, the Edwardian Era. George V, you may argue, put the clock back and refused to march with the times; but it is not a monarch's role to be radical, and at his death the British Empire was larger and more influential than it had ever been. The old boy may have been blimpish and blinkered in many things, but he was still an apt figurehead for the times. Europe itself, after all, made no real progress during his reign – which was why the Second World War had to be fought.

Edward VIII might have been a brilliant monarch in other times. Had he reigned during the twenties or the 'Swinging Sixties', for instance, he would have made a notable contribution; but with Britain being drawn into the austere forties of hardship and bloodshed, his charisma would have been all wrong. As it was, the gallant amateur efforts of George VI proved utterly right.

The start of the fifties in Britain saw a new spirit at work in the land. Rationing was over, new goods were appearing in the shops; the country was gradually settling for a mild kind of welfare socialism, and although abroad Britain could not rival the power of America, she was still one of the Big Five. She might not wield as much industrial clout, but by God she had moral influence!

And a new Queen, too.

The accession of little Princess Elizabeth – so young, so ethereally pretty – to the throne of Britain was heralded as the start of a new Elizabethan Age. There would be a plethora of poets and explorers, just as there had been in the days of Good Queen

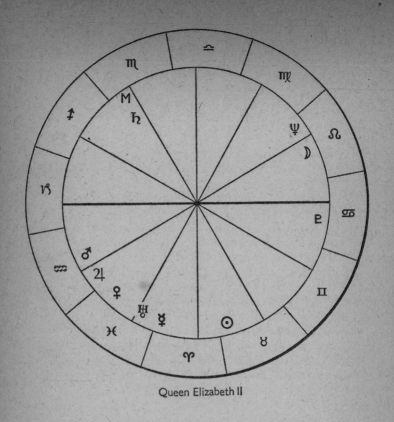

Queen Elizabeth II

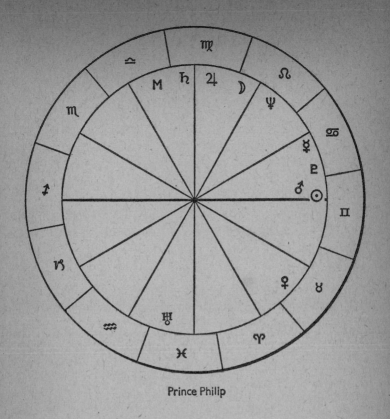

Prince Philip

Bess. Naturally, the young Queen would not be as cantankerous and meddlesome as her sixteenth-century namesake. No, the new reign would be an inspiration to the people of Britain at a more sublime spiritual level.

Now, twenty-five years later, nobody talks of an Elizabethan Age any more. It was a fiction all along, a piece of blowsy romance that would have borne no relevance to the twentieth century if it had ever come to pass. But has the reality of Queen Elizabeth II been any more relevant? Has her personality embodied the qualities of the British people through the fifties, sixties and seventies of this turbulent century?

What she has sought to do, in accordance with her temperament and outlook, is to act as the rock-hard foundation stone of a society undergoing deep, irrevocable changes. She sees herself as the repository of those essential virtues that should be the basis of any civilized community. She is a traditionalist because she respects the experience of the past.

All this is entirely consistent with her horoscope. If I had been asked to devise a birth-chart for a constitutional monarch who would act as a bulwark against change, I could not have invented a more appropriate configuration than 21 April 1926 at 1.40 a.m. in London!

This makes Capricorn her Ascendant. Capricorn the goat – and there are two kinds of goat in nature, just as there are two types of Capricorn-rising people. The first is the domestic breed – patient, unadventurous, eating its allotted patch of grass whether or not it is yoked, a good servant to its owner but rather too . . . well, uncuddly to be a real friend to anyone. The second is the mountain variety, hopping from crag to crag in its search for the summit. This is the ambitious goat, independent, able and willing to endure the loneliness at the top of the world.

In human terms, the one kind of goat is personified in the civil servant – anonymous, efficient, the power behind the Throne. The other is the managing director, the self-made entrepreneur who doesn't need a committee to make decisions for him. In both cases, *power* is the name of the game.

Her Majesty, like most Capricorn-rising people, combines both kinds of goat in her outer temperament, though the civil servant predominates. She has a slightly frosty face at the best of times, and everything she does, even in private life, has an air of caution and responsibility about it. You feel that she cannot totally let her hair down. It is not simply her office that forbids it, but her basic outlook on life. She is held back by invisible chains of her own making.

Every Capricorn-rising person is also a midwinter person, for Capricorn is associated with the cold season when food is scarce and must be eked out with stony fairness to all. Capricorn-rising people are desperately thrifty. Even when they are surrounded by luxury, their minds are fixed on the poverty that could be just around the corner. Even if Elizabeth had been born in more sumptuous days when royal finances were not constantly questioned, she would still have been economical in her needs. Leaving aside the gorgeous trappings needed by any Head of State, Queen or President or whomever, Her Majesty does not surround herself with fabulous possessions. Her taste is traditionally British upper-class, with a liking for Regency and early Victorian furniture, muted pastel colours, good but not showy paintings, and clothes which have a timeless elegance rather than an immediate trendy impact. Obviously her environment is a good deal more palatial than the vast majority of her subjects enjoy, but she is living among the glories of the past instead of being extravagant herself.

The Queen keeps a tight control over the spending of other royal figures, too, especially her own children. She may not have direct influence over the Duchy of Cornwall estates, for instance, which provides much of the income of the Prince of Wales, nor the Civil List provisions by which Parliament pays the Royal Family expenses, but by example and upbringing she has taught her offspring to be thrifty. It's hard for Princess Anne, a Leo girl, to be as tight with the purse-strings as her mother, but she's been trained the hard way.

With Capricorn as her Ascendant, Saturn is the ruling planet in Elizabeth's birth-chart. It lies on the edge of her Eleventh House, to do with friendships in general and one's ability to mix with others in clubs, societies and associations of all kinds. Now the fact that her ruling planet lies there signifies that the Queen places great importance on these kinds of gathering, though in her case it is not a question of popping down to the local bingo club! Her faith is fixed on the British Commonwealth and the various associations for which she is patron or president. But, because the planet is heavy, dutiful Saturn, it follows that the Queen is a somewhat reluctant mixer herself. She does her duty, without greatly enjoying herself. And this applies to her whole career as well, for this planet Saturn also lies exactly due south in her horoscope – in conjunction with the Midheaven, which signifies her overall destiny in life.

Saturn on the Midheaven means that the Queen performs all her duties in an over-serious mood. Her smile is occasionally wan. Beneath it lies tedium and probably a hard-done-by feeling that she is putting herself out for all these cheering, waving crowds and that she is not properly appreciated in return. Certainly, in her heart, there are times when she wishes she did not have to meet yet another newly arrived Ambassador or perform yet another ceremonial opening. But, deeper still, in her heart of hearts, she is most unwilling to abandon any of her responsibilities. By temperament she is a clinger, a survivor at all costs. I cannot see her easily abdicating the Throne in favour of her son, Prince Charles, unless it can be clearly shown that such an act would be the ultimate duty of all. She clings out of principle – not greed or selfishness.

She learnt this devotion to duty from her adored father George. It is fascinating to note that George's Moon (in Scorpio, remember, providing that inner grit and stamina) occupied the same degree of the Zodiac where Elizabeth's Saturn–Midheaven conjunction lay at her birth. His demeanour – the most natural and unforced element in his character – provided the inspiration for Elizabeth in her career as Princess and later as monarch.

There is an equally close, warm contact between the horoscopes of mother and daughter. The Queen Mother, as we have seen, has her Sun in the twelfth degree of Leo, exactly where the Queen's Moon lies. Whenever you find such a Sun–Moon conjunction between the generations, you find a deep, almost inexpressible bond of mutual interests and outlook. If the Queen absorbed a sense of duty from her father, she inherited gaiety and a love of simple family warmth from her mother. We must distinguish between Her Majesty's public smile, which is only sincere in a leaden, dutiful way, and her private countenance, represented by her Moon in Leo in the Seventh House, which is much more light-hearted. Naturally the two get in each other's way at times. She can rarely forget she is the Queen, even with her own children. She has a deep, ingrained pride, and any kind of teasing (from her husband, perhaps) will quickly bring a hurt rebuke.

This sign of Leo plays a deeply interesting role in the modern Royal Family. It is conspicuous by its absence from the horoscopes of earlier royal figures examined in previous chapters. Only with the entry of Queen Elizabeth the Queen Mother to the Royal Family does Leo make a significant appearance. Clearly her Scottish dash and spirit has enlivened the old Hanoverian line and brought a touch of genuine royal élan back into the British Royal Family – for, make no mistake about it, Leo is traditionally known as the royal sign, dating right back to the earliest days of astrology in the time of the Chaldeans and Egyptians.

Of course the Leonian notion of kingship harks back to the grand old days of Sun-worship. You see the same manifestation in King Louis XIV of France, known as the Sun-king. Louis wanted to be the fount of all honour and power in France, and in return he expected his subjects to be wildly affectionate and adoring towards him. In just the same way, modern sunbathers expect the Sun to pour warmth and sensual well-being into their bodies, and give nothing in return except gratitude. All very undemocratic, in the sense the sunbathers cannot switch on the Sun or alter its power in any way.

Our own Crown, on the other hand, is striving to stay abreast of modern social changes. Being a hereditary title, it cannot be made into a truly democratic institution, of course, but in its behaviour and interests the Royal Family seeks to reflect the desires and aspirations of Britons in the 1970s. This is why I find it odd, to say the least, that Leo is so important in the astrology of the present royal figures. The opposite sign, Aquarius, which was important in the chart of the 'modern' Edward VIII, is the part of the Zodiac that you might expect to play a significant role.

As it is, Leo occupies a crucial role in the horoscope of the Queen Mother, her two daughters, her son-in-law Prince Philip and three of his four children: Charles, Anne and Andrew.

It suggests that our Royal Family is composed of people in the entertainment industry rather than true power, politics and prestige. They are glamorous 'personalities' to be loved for their charisma rather than their inherent power to govern. There is a side to their characters that enjoys being fêted and cheered. They are capable of being vain. And they are susceptible of being flattered – some not as much as others, of course, but all of them to some degree.

This, at any rate, is a somewhat cynical estimation of the Leo influence in their lives. At a more sublime level, it is possible that some ancient spiritual power is being channelled through these otherwise rather ordinary individuals – perhaps the most ancient and venerable power of all which first kindled human life into existence on this planet Earth.

I mentioned earlier that the Queen is a Rock of Ages to which, hopefully, the British people can attach themselves, metaphorically speaking, in times of stress and rapid changes of value. This four-square stance, reminiscent of the mythical character John Bull, comes from the Queen's Sun in Taurus, whose symbol, indeed, is the bull. She has the bull's slow, patient manner, gently chewing away at experience to get the best possible value from it, toiling in a steady routine with the yoke of responsibilities fixed firmly across its shoulders, always aware of long-term requirements and needing to have a meadow of its own where it can feel at home.

The Queen, too, needs the right pasture in which to put down emotional roots. She is a countrywoman at heart, a soul in need of the regular rhythm of the seasons. She works at nature's pace. She hates being hurried and chivvied from one appointment to the next. While her husband Philip may pause too long with one person, or dart off in some spur-of-the-moment enthusiasm that throws the whole schedule out of kilter, the Queen is much more time-conscious and even-paced in her habits.

Another powerful Taurean motivation in life is the need to be *constructive*. Even a power-crazed man such as Hitler (who, like the Queen, had the Sun at 0° Taurus) was intent on constructing the Third Reich, even though he seemed to be destroying a great deal in the process. The Queen is wholly constructive. She seeks to build bridges between the peoples of the world. She has built a firm foundation in her own marriage and family life. And she has always found it hard to tear down the past. When a Taurean builds, the fabric is meant to endure, in the words of Adolf Hitler, at least 'for a thousand years' and preferably for eternity.

To reinforce the Queen's attachment to age, tradition and the pull of the past, the Sun in her horoscope lies in the Fourth House to do with home, family and the influence of parental values. She is a natural conservative, quite independently of her class, station and constitutional position. There is nothing in her chart that tempts her to look forward greatly to the future – nothing, that is, except a Mars–Jupiter conjunction in Aquarius. This suggests to me that in other circumstances, the Queen would have made a good scientist, not so much in the exact sciences such as physics or mathematics so much as natural history, perhaps, or archaeology. She is interested in finding solutions to problems, and I believe she likes modern gadgets. At a fantasy level, she may have more than a passing interest in science fiction, but I cannot see her wanting to become Britain's first woman astronaut!

This Mars–Jupiter conjunction is exactly opposed by Neptune and squared by Saturn and the Midheaven. This indicates that she is a frustrated businesswoman, though for all we know she may take a strong interest in the way her personal investments increase in value through the years. If she had not been born a Princess, I believe she would have thrived as a career girl. Cautious on the surface, she would have enjoyed taking entrepreneurial risks. The most obvious fields of endeavour for Mrs Mountbatten, as she would have been, are farming (especially stock breeding), horse-training, estate management (though I don't think she's sly enough to be an *estate agent!*) and, most obviously of all, hotel and catering work. Yes, Elizabeth Mountbatten would be quite a formidable guest-house owner, spick and span in her habits and serving good, if unspicy food. All bills would need to be paid promptly, and there would be NO hanky-panky allowed in the bedrooms!

As it is, she has inherited the family firm and is making sure it remains a going concern.

It is very hard to imagine Philip Mountbatten as a hotelier – indeed, as *anything* requiring single-minded application. He is a royal Figaro, a Jack o' All Trades turning his capable hand to any worthwhile project that interests him. He could no more settle to an ordinary nine-till-five occupation than . . . well, blow up the Houses of Parliament. He needs variety in all the work he tackles and has great enterprise.

He is the only major royal figure since Queen Alexandra for whom we do not have an accurate horoscope. Like her, he was born into a slightly down-at-heel section of European royalty – in his case, the Greeks, who were of course Danes, and indeed related to the British Royal Family in numerous little connections – and, like Alix, his actual birthday, 10 June 1921, is unsung in royal annals: no bulletins, no crowds at the palace gates, just the local doctor delivering the baby on the dining-room table of Mon Repos, Corfu. The time is 'believed to be sunset'.

Like Alix, too, Philip burst on the British royal scene in a fresh, slightly unconventional way. Both of them married monarchs with Saturn strong in their charts, but both of them were able to stand up for themselves and bring a note of *spontaneity* to the somewhat drab surroundings in which they found themselves. Alix coped with an irate, overbearing husband who needed freedom. Philip has coped with the reverse situation: a faithful, somewhat strict spouse with a strong sense of responsibility. Alix needed to retain her self-respect as a married woman; Philip has needed to keep his self-esteem as an ambitious and energetic man of action.

Given that Philip's purported birth-time is approximately correct, there are three possible Ascendants. He would have Scorpio rising if he was born a couple of hours before sunset – but no one can imagine that this warm, genial, adventurous man could have such a secretive, intense Zodiac sign for his Ascendant. If he was born an hour or more after dark, the rising sign would be Capricorn – again too serious and heavy an outer temperament for dashing Prince Philip. No, there can be no doubt whatever; Philip's Ascendant must be Sagittarius, the same as King Edward VII's. Both men have the same outgoing personality – versatile, challenging, inquisitive, never taking 'no' for an answer. In Philip's case, the whole appearance is irresistibly Sagittarian: the elongated bullet head, the profile sharp as a scimitar, the crisp, clean jawline and sweep of intelligent forehead and those long, lean legs made for jumping astride a horse and riding off cowboy-fashion into the sunset . . .

Every Sagittarius-rising person is a born preacher. Philip likes to lay down the law, not in a hard-and-fast way but because he enjoys the sound of his own voice and loves to stir up controversy and comment. He has an obsessive desire to be honest, at least with himself. He doesn't suffer fools gladly, and has no time for stupidity, inefficiency or deviousness. And he has a wonderful sense of the ridiculous, which makes him a natural humorist. His children Charles and Anne have been brought up in the same spirit, but with them there is a slightly forced note about their *bon mots*. Philip has the right relaxed touch.

Above all, he has great buoyancy of temperament. He flares up in anger, but never bears resentment. As soon as he's bored, he moves on to a new interest. He's a great exhorter – to British schoolchildren climbing mountains or emergent African nations or businessmen abroad or any of the hundreds of specialized groups in which he takes a personal concern. He's a great cheerer-up, too.

The pity, from his personal point of view, is that he's never had the opportunity to make a single gigantic contribution. Astrologically the reason is that the dreaded planet Saturn is probably hovering near his Midheaven, preventing him from feeling the full flush of achievement, however much other people may feel he has done in his lifetime. But I do not think he hankers for *power* in the way that a politician or managing director does. His ruling planet Jupiter, after all, probably lies in the Ninth House, concerned with travel and higher education. Philip's primary aim in life is – or should be – to explore, to widen his horizons, to spread the word, to search after knowledge and enlightenment. The eternal traveller enjoys no ultimate satisfaction, for there is always another road to tramp, another journey to be made.

This is the great difference between the Queen and Prince

Philip. She is honestly content to stay in the same place all her life – Balmoral for preference, or Sandringham as a second choice. Her journeys abroad are State occasions, with the odd foray into France or Germany to stay with old friends or relations. She would never holiday away from Britain, for instance.

Philip would, if he knew what a holiday was. But he rarely relaxes. As a Geminian, he must be mentally on the move all the time.

Part of this energy comes from a conjunction between the Sun and Mars in Gemini. These two 'masculine' planets side by side make Philip very much a man's man. His love of sport stems from this conjunction, and so does his swiftness of thought and decisiveness of action. So, above all, does his famous temper, which is not true irascibility at all but an explosion of frustrated rage whenever people – or circumstances – do not behave in a sensible, straightforward manner. We have seen how George VI burned bright in the heat of battle when the Sun and Mars formed a conjunction in his horoscope during 1916. Well, Philip is like that all the time: red-hot, non-stop royal incandescence.

As far as the Royal Family is concerned, he is the last of the Geminians. Victoria, George V and Queen Mary, the Duchess of Windsor and Prince Philip – a mixed bunch, on the face of it, with apparently little in common. Yet each of them has been a Geminian at heart. None of them ever quite grew up – even Philip, who has retained a youthful freshness of outlook until well into his fifties. Perhaps it is this child-like quality which has made them such good royal servants of Britain. People who act as constitutional figureheads must not be too clever or power-hungry. They must play their chosen role in much the same way that an actor must subdue his own personality in order to portray a character on stage. The Royals, in point of fact, must play several roles at the same time – dignified State figures, ideal family types, good-humoured and kindly guests at local functions, and so forth. It is striking that the two most prevalent Zodiac signs represented on royal horoscopes – Gemini and Leo – are those most closely allied with the theatrical profession.

In Philip's own case, he exhibits the Geminian's ease and love of moving from the sublime to the ridiculous in one fell swoop. He shows his maturity in being able to do this without mockery. He can relax a stiff formal occasion with a joke or ironic comment and still maintain the dignity of the event. Quite obviously he has the Geminian's gift of words, for no other royal figure has ever *enjoyed* speechifying as much as Philip. He can slip with adroitness into any number of royal roles, which is an example of the Geminian adaptability, and he loves keeping his hands busy: gesturing, taking photographs, painting, playing sport. The famous Philip stance – leaning intently forward whilst clasping the hands behind the back – is a trick he unconsciously employs to keep those hands still on State occasions.

He's such a ubiquitous chap in British life, popping up in every facet of cultural, scientific, industrial and sporting affairs, that it's easy to forget he's only here because he's married to the Queen. If they had never fallen in love, he might simply be Admiral Mountbatten by now. His family connections with the British royalty would have been too distant to allow him to perform any official duties like a Governor-Generalship, for instance, and too close to allow him to enter government. If the Royal Navy proved too restricting – and he is a Geminian man of parts – he might well have taken a Golden Handshake in the 1957 reorganization and . . . what? Gone into business? Or industry? Or one of those international agencies like UNO, FAO or UNESCO? He would have made a good roving ambassador – or better still, a roving troubleshooter flying to distant shores to sort out a little local difficulty.

As it is, he's His Royal Highness. Philip and Elizabeth first met in his Dartmouth days during the war, but the romance blossomed in 1946 and the next year they were married. For Elizabeth, with her stolid Earthy temperament, it was love at virtually first sight, and it's impossible to believe that she has ever looked at anyone else. Loyalty and the need for security are absolutely built into her horoscope and character.

Philip's horoscope is different. Sagittarius rising and the Sun in Gemini make for a highly restless personality. He may have the Sun square Saturn, making him aware of the *need* to exercise responsibility, but the temptation always remains to go off at a tangent. This is likely to apply as much to his social life as his career, for the planet of love, Venus, forms an easy and harmonious trine with the variety-seeking Jupiter. This accounts for his charm and relaxed manner with everyone. With girls, it would tend to make him most personable. Besides, the Sun–Mars conjuction makes him a manly character.

Whether he has ever strayed from grace depends as much on opportunity as desire. What's more, a man does not necessarily live out his innate character. He can exercise discipline, which sounds repressive, but better still he can divert his variety-seeking mood away from one outlet (sex) towards a multitude of others, and naturally a Geminian is adept at this psychological sleight of hand.

Sometimes it is hard to know how deeply a Geminian ever feels about anything. He tends to talk himself into love, and this may have been specially true of Philip, as the Sun had moved by direction to form a conjunction with the talkative Geminian planet Mercury when he became engaged. Courtship, wedding and settling into the royal way of life cannot have been easy for him, for by the next year his Moon had moved to form a conjunction with Saturn.

All this time, young Elizabeth herself was deliciously happy, with the blissful planet Jupiter moving to conjunction with her planet of love, Venus. A couple of years later, Mars had arrived at the same point, signifying an emotionally fulfilling time, and this corresponded with the birth of Prince Charles.

There must have been frequent moments of stress between Elizabeth and Philip. There is nothing in his horoscope which is sympathetic towards her tough Capricorn Ascendant, and nothing in hers that fully understands and appreciates his own Geminian character. But marriages do not necessarily work well between so-called 'compatible' people. It is frequently an advantage to marry someone with an opposite temperament, provided there is basic love and respect for each other, for out of this friction can develop the grit that bonds the couple together. Philip has clearly acted as a warm, stimulating companion to

Elizabeth. By my calculations, his Ascendant will lie very close to the Sagittarian Sun of his father-in-law, George VI, and Elizabeth, always a girl in need of a strong father-figure, will have sensed the similarity between the two men. In addition, Elizabeth and Philip share a Moon in Leo, and there is a wonderfully ardent trine contact between his Mars and her Jupiter (always the best indicator of a good relationship, as it is his manhood, Mars, which awakens her enthusiasm, Jupiter).

The famous, and frequently dismissed, phrase 'My husband and I' has never quite rung true of Elizabeth and Philip. George and Mary, or for that matter George and Elizabeth, seemed more of a natural couple, while our present monarch and her consort remain individuals in their own right who happen to be married to each other. Perhaps the reason here is not so much astrological incompatability – though that plays a part – as the gender of monarch. Despite the protestations of Women's Libbers, most people still think of the Crown as a symbol of male authority. With a king on the throne, his marriage partner is a natural and acceptable adjunct to the central figurehead. With a queen, however, the consort is placed in a much more difficult position. Because his wife takes precedence and receives the attention, the man must inevitably play the part of 'supporting cast', and this can be damaging to his self-esteem. A hundred years ago, the Prince Consort loathed his second-rate position, and did everything he could to encroach upon Queen Victoria's power. As a result, at his premature death she felt defenceless and utterly alone. In the present reign, Philip has been much more sensible, never attempting to usurp the Queen's constitutional role and always one step behind Her Majesty, so to speak, when they are together in public. It must have been a galling experience for a man of such vibrant egoism (which is not the same as selfishness, of course, nor vanity). And in years to come, the position will become worse, for his role as Top Male in the Royal Family must be abandoned in favour of the Heir Apparent, Prince Charles.

It will be a measure of Prince Philip's maturity that he yield this position with grace and deference. As a Geminian, he knows how to change his position, and should have no difficulty. But the Queen is another matter. Despite her charm, she is a formidable woman with great Taurean obstinacy. Will she yield her power, voluntarily before her death, and usher in the reign of Good King Charles?

Charles and ——?

Prince Charles is an enigma. On the face of it, he is a young man with a cleancut modern outlook on life. He is the first heir to the throne to have benefited from straightforward schooling methods with other children. He has been brought up in a relaxed, unneurotic household, which is more than can be said of the last King of England, his grandfather George. Today he leads an active, well-balanced life – his time shared between his naval duties and his obligations as a leading member of the Royal Family. All in all, he seems thoroughly normal.

But a big question-mark hangs over his future. He has been groomed since childhood to play the part of the acceptable prince – an Establishment figure who nonetheless possesses the common touch, a man who will embody the essentially 'English' virtues, a constitutional monarch without any mystery or mystique attached to him. This, at least, is the present concept of kingship evolved by the Queen, Prince Philip and their palace advisers. But it was not so when Charles was born, on a foggy November 14th, a year after his parent's wedding, at 9.14 p.m. in London. In those early years, there was still a very patronizing attitude by British royalty towards their Scandinavian counterparts. Riding about on bicycles might be all right for the Low Countries, but Britain, with her rich heritage of pageantry, etc., etc., deserved something better.

Since then, the Crown has sought to keep up with changes in public opinion – and one of the first aspects of royalty to disappear has been the veneration formerly accorded to the monarch. The British public is principally interested nowadays in bread and circuses – or, put another way, money and entertainment. So long as the Royal Family does not cost too much and provides a touch of spectacle on State occasions – as well as provide copy for gossip columns – it will be tolerated and even enjoyed. But if it ever becomes too expensive or, worse still, boring, it will go the way of the Church of England: a quaint anachronism that will be ever so gently ignored into extinction.

In Britain, republicanism will grow out of apathy rather than rebellion.

This, at any rate, is a credible scenario for the rest of this century: the Royal Family increasingly being by-passed because they serve no obviously compelling purpose in life. But there remain the deeper needs of a community, and these can easily be forgotten in easy peace-time conditions. In times of crisis, a Head of State is required to be the flesh-and-blood manifestation of those basic virtues – goodness, sincerity, valour, confidence – which a besieged people wish to summon within themselves. A monarch must fulfil this ancient atavistic function if he is ever to play his part to the full.

This is the ambivalent situation in which Prince Charles finds himself. On the one hand, he must be a glamorous but self-deprecating man of the people providing some fairly cheap entertainment value to keep the tourists happy; on the other, he must hold himself in readiness to fulfil his mythic role as leader of the people, if need be.

It's almost as though the future Charles III must find the balance between Charles II, who saw the monarchy as a branch of the entertainment industry, and Charles I, who tragically overestimated his own position as a divinely appointed ruler of his peoples.

This balancing act is neatly illustrated in his horoscope. His surface temperament, shown by the Ascendant, is the warmly theatrical sign of Leo. His inner character, to which Charles will increasingly lean as he gains in age and maturity, is shown by his Sun-sign: the introspective, powerful and brooding Scorpio.

Both signs are Fixed, and so, for good measure, is his Moon-sign, Taurus; so Charles resembles his mother more than his father. He is strong, resolute, even a shade stubborn at times. He is inclined to maintain a state of affairs rather than change it or replace it with something else. He can concentrate like mad, and has a much

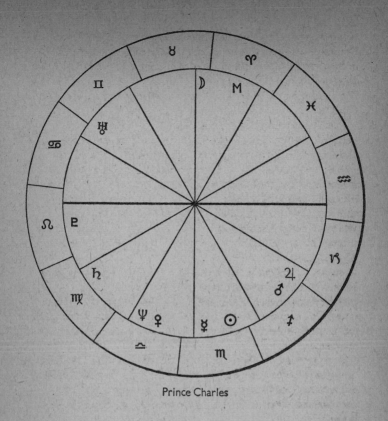

Prince Charles

greater natural ability than his father to apply himself diligently to unpleasant tasks. He may not be so successful, but he does try.

Let's start with his Leo Ascendant. This makes him an affectionate and strong-minded young man. He needs to be in the limelight, not so much because he wants to show off but due to his inner belief that the centre of the stage is simply the right place for him. He needs to take charge of a situation and exercise some measure of leadership. He likes to formulate plans, give orders and delegate responsibilities.

Every Leo-rising individual has more than his fair share of pride. A nice word for this is self-respect; a nasty one is arrogance. Charles has been taught, at home, his school Gordonstoun, and the Officers' Mess in the Royal Navy, to encourage self-respect and play down arrogance and vanity. But it can't always be easy. Charles is simply not a particularly humble man. It is relatively easy in his position, where the eyes of the world are focused – for the most part affectionately – on him, to make little jokes about all the royal publicity and to make it plain that he wants to be just one of the lads. But in other, adverse circumstances – if he were unemployed, for instance, or down-and-out – he would lose his bloom of self-confidence and desperately seek some way of making himself important in the eyes of others. When the Sun shines, the world seems a happy, natural paradise, but a single cloud can obscure the sunlight and turn this world into a grey, depressed place. In just the same way, it's bonny Prince Charlie for most of the time; but every so often a cloud of weariness, self-doubt or personal disappointment will hide the bright gaiety of his soul. And there's no half-way stage. When Charles gets low, he probably gets very low indeed, though as a Scorpian he can mask his moods from people quite close to him.

This Leo Ascendant is very near the Queen Mother's charming Mercury–Venus conjunction. Charles and his grandmother are extremely close. From her he has inherited a sense of grace, certainly a love of music and art, and affable good manners. Whereas Pappa Philip can be blunt to the point of rudeness, Charles is much more cautious in his dealings with others. He does not go out of his way to stir up trouble.

The ruler of his chart is the Sun, which lies in Scorpio in the

Fourth House, to do with home, family and inherited values. This is the same House-position as the Sun in his mother's horoscope. Both of them, monarch and monarch-to-be, have this staunch respect for the past, especially their own Royal Family. Charles is deeply interested in history, for he believes it contains valuable lessons for the present age. When he marries and has children of his own, he will be a loving husband and father.

I mentioned earlier that there is a direct astrological 'line of descent' between George VI's Moon in the third decanate of Scorpio and Elizabeth's Midheaven. Now we find that Charles's Sun lies in the same part of the Zodiac. This makes it strongly likely that Charles will indeed ascend to the Throne in due course. I say this, because several earlier astrologers have claimed that for one reason or another – assassination, illness, accident or revolution – he will never be King.

Appropriately for a young naval officer, Scorpio is said to be the Zodiac sign of the Navy. This means that all Scorpians, to a greater or less extent, are motivated by the Jack Hawkins–Ealing Films syndrome, which means a stiff upper lip in the face of the hurricane, a calm fearless image even though they may be inwardly as churned up as the raging seas outside, and a general absence of overt emotion. Scorpians love stress and crisis, even though they swear blind that all they want is the quiet, peaceful life. Not a bit of it. They are ineluctably drawn towards drama and life-or-death situations. They have quite a curiosity about death itself and the innermost workings of the mind. In other circumstances, Charles would make an admirable doctor specializing in mental illness. He has the kind of brain that loves unearthing mysteries and discovering the real truth about an enigmatic state of affairs.

I called Charles an enigma, so clearly one of his most absorbing hobbies is self-criticism. Every Scorpian is introspective and self-doubting at times. Charles is certainly a self-improver. He will measure his actions according to his own high standards. No Scorpian can ever take life easily. There has to be a struggle of some kind.

There will often be a clash between the Leo and Scorpio sides of his character. He resembles one of those old-style barometers where the lady with the parasol pops out when it's fair weather (Leo) to be replaced by the gent with the brolly when rain threatens (Scorpio). But he is excellent at hiding his real feelings, so no casual observer will be able to spot whether he feels sunny or sodden at any particular time.

One thing is certain: if his heart is ever broken, he will keep his emotions to himself, but he will never truly recover from the loss.

The third important actor in Charles's horoscope is his Moon, situated in exactly the same part of the sky as his mother's Sun – in Taurus, in fact. Here again is this vivid astrological 'inheritance' at work. At an ordinary human level, it means that mother and son are astonishingly close in emotional rapport. This may not always be comfortable for them. They may know each other too well, and in his adolescence Prince Charles may have resented this unconscious intrusion into his inner heart.

In his own personality, this Taurean Moon gives Charles a deep instinctive love of the English countryside. It provides him with a robust constitution and a relish for the good things in life: food and drink, companionship, love-making. It definitely adds to his conservatism of outlook.

There is a further vivid link with earlier generations. Charles's Mars is conjunct George VI's Sun and opposite Prince Philip's Sun. At a sporty, energetic, courageous level, this pulls the three men together, and may, for all we know, signify a strong transmission of spiritual energy down through the Royal Family.

There are two questions uppermost in people's minds when considering Prince Charles's future. What kind of King will he make? And who will be his Queen?

First of all, he has the innate self-respect, dignity and sense of integrity which are obviously required of a monarch. Leo-rising people have a powerful awareness of honour, which is part of their built-in pride. They hate doing anything underhand or cheap.

What's more, Charles is not a selfish man. He may hate to be on the fringe of the crowd, preferring to be the centre of attention, but he puts the needs of the crowd before his own.

He'll be a popular king, for he has plenty of easy, unforced charm. His Sun lies exactly between Venus and Jupiter, the two beneficial planets, so he radiates a gently warming charisma –

exactly what's needed from a figurehead of his sort. Admittedly his Scorpio Sun does make it hard for him to enjoy small talk; he will always tend towards the serious kind of conversation. But he's an approachable man.

His Scorpian qualities give him excellent control in a crisis. It is unlikely that an unscrupulous Prime Minister will be able to sway him away from his duty. Charles himself cannot be devious, so there is no danger that he will meddle in politics.

He sounds a paragon of virtue. What, then, are his faults?

As he gets older, he may get out of sympathy with the younger generation. This is specially true if the monarchy becomes seriously ignored in the 1990s. His lack of political *nous* could then be a handicap rather than an advantage. Saturn on the cusp of the Second House indicates problems with money, and there could be a campaign to confiscate the family fortune which would turn him overnight into an obstinate and resentful middle-aged man.

One further problem – not so much a personality defect as a difficult state of affairs which he may bungle – is hinted at in the exact Jupiter–Uranus opposition. This resembles a crackle of lightning every once in a while striking the sturdy oak tree. Sooner or later, the stolidity of the tree (Charles's character) is going to be struck down by a momentary electric storm (a crisis, accident, sudden turn of events). The first time this was activated was at the ceremony at Caenarvon Castle proclaiming him Prince of Wales. There were fears for his life from Welsh nationalist extremists, and talk of calling off the ritual, though everything passed off peacefully on the day. The next important time is the late 1980s. Prince Andrew, more of a rebel than his elder brother, will be affected by the same astrological state of affairs as Charles, and could even be the cause of Charles's problems.

Uranus, of course, is the planet symbolizing Charles's marriage, since it rules his Seventh House. The fact that Jupiter opposes it suggests to me that Charles will look for an enthusiastic, buoyant kind of girl, quite possibly foreign and perhaps American, since Jupiter is strongly associated with the United States. His uncle, Lord Snowdon, says that Charles likes his girls 'blonde and busty', which certainly seems to be what his Leo Ascendant would prefer; but physical attraction alone cannot be the principal factor affecting his choice of wife. His more serious Scorpio character makes him want a deep, meaningful relationship. And his wife will become Queen of England, so by temperament and perhaps training she needs to know how to fulfil the arduous duties of the job. 'The one advantage about marrying a princess, for instance,' he has said, 'or somebody from a royal family, is that they know what happens.'

Unfortunately for Charles, there are relatively few eligible princesses left in the world. The short list would seem to consist of three:

Princess Marie Christine daughter of King Leopold III of Belgium and his English-born wife Princess Lilian. Born 6 February 1951. She's an ultra-cool girl with Sun and Moon in the rational sign of Aquarius. Lots of good humour and charm, thanks to a Venus–Jupiter conjunction, and very lively and forthright and adventurous, due to an exact Mars–Jupiter conjunction. There's a Sun–Pluto opposition in her horoscope, suggesting that there could be a big turning-point in her destiny, but there's no real indication whether it's good or bad and anyway is unlikely to be triggered into action for another fifteen years, in the early 1990s.

There aren't any stunning links between Charles and Marie Christine, though she seems an attractive and straightforward girl without any deep hang-ups.

Princess Marie Astrid daughter of the Grand Duke Jean of Luxembourg. Born 17 February 1954. Another Aquarian, this time with the Moon in Leo (linking with Charles's Ascendant) Mars in Sagittarius (same as Charles) and Jupiter forming a nice harmonious trine with Charles's planet of love Venus. This is another cleancut, uncomplex horoscope, and there could be plenty of warmth and light-hearted rapport between them. One drawback is that her Saturn conjoins his Mercury: an indication of possible mental conflicts. She might keep secrets from him, or there could be a disparity in their willingness to concentrate on the same interests together.

Princess Caroline of Monaco, daughter of Prince Rainier and Princess Grace. Born 23 January 1957. Yet *another* Aquarian:

European royalty seems very modern and democratic in its younger generation. Caroline is a real possibility, believe it or not, despite her rebellious and independent nature. She has a close Sun–Uranus opposition lying exactly on Charles's Ascendant-Descendant axis. There's no doubt that her personality will stir Charles up, though it's more a short exciting relationship than a quiet, long-lasting marriage. She has a sweet Mercury–Venus conjunction (like the Queen Mum) so she'd be able to handle herself graciously on formal occasions. Her Mars forms a super sexy conjunction with his Moon, and best of all, her Jupiter absolutely bisects his own Jupiter–Uranus opposition signifying a possible foreign marriage. And to cap it all, her Moon lies in Scorpio, linking up nicely with his own Sun.

Certainly this would be a glamorous marriage. Caroline is a tough-minded girl who might find it hard to obey Charles and the palace advisers on every point. But she is lucky and good-humoured, and though she may not be blonde she's certainly busty!

The chief drawback, with all these foreign princesses, is that they are Roman Catholics, and by the Act of 1689 he is not allowed to marry anyone professing that religion. It's doubtful whether many British subjects care tuppence nowadays about the religious scruples of 300 years ago, but Charles would need to be very much in love in order to force a new Act through Parliament.

If we turn to home-grown products, the list obviously becomes longer, but there are four girls whom Charles has regularly escorted who seem – so far – to stand out from the rest:

Lady Charlotte Manners daughter of the Duke of Rutland. Born 7 January 1947. Sun in Capricorn, Moon in Cancer – so an ambitious and emotionally conservative girl with a strong respect for traditional values. The nicest contact between them is a conjunction between her Jupiter and his Sun, which means they are capable of being good *friends* all their lives. She also has a fiery Sun–Mars conjunction contacting his Venus, which is sexy, with a touch of hostility and jealousy thrown in. The nastiest contact is the presence of her Saturn on his Ascendant. Her frosty Capricorn nature will sometimes try to snuff out Charles's natural Leo warmth. She probably tends to be a little more cynical than he is ... more world-weary.

Angela Nevill daughter of one of the Queen's oldest friends, Rupert Nevill. Born 2 January 1948. Another Capricorn. An old friend she may be, but I can't see Angela becoming the Queen. There are relatively few points of contact between her horoscope and Charles's, and one of these is a sharp little conjunction in Virgo between his Saturn and her Mars. He turns a cold shoulder (Saturn), in other words, to the idea of being the man in her life (Mars).

Caroline Longman daughter of Lady Elizabeth Longman. Born 24 December 1951. Oh dear, yet *another* Capricorn! Prince Charles seems to draw his girl-friends, or would-be girl-friends, exclusively from the midwinter signs of Capricorn and Aquarius. But Caroline is a real possibility. She has her Moon in Scorpio (linking with Charles's Sun) and there's a lovely trine between her Jupiter and his Ascendant. More important still, his Venus is practically in exact conjunction with his Sun (so this could be a real love match) and her Mars is precisely in line with his Venus (making it a very sweetly sexy liaison as well). Caroline would be a capable wife and mother and a Queen of firm determination. It's worth bearing in mind that Charles's view of his wife-to-be is bound to be coloured by his image of his mother – not because he's a mother's boy himself but due to the fact that Her Majesty has provided him with a living daily example of what a Queen should be like. So Caroline's Capricorn Sun fits neatly with the Queen's Capricorn Ascendant. These two women should learn to respect each other.

Davina Sheffield glamorous orphan who has attracted the most attention so far. Born 1 March 1951. She's a restless, easy-going Piscean with an adventurous Moon in Sagittarius. Not desperately loyal and steadfast, and with a Venus-Uranus square she's liable to develop sudden little romantic fancies on the spur of the moment. Her Mars exactly bisects Charles's Jupiter-Uranus opposition, which accounts for the strong physical ties between them. What's really striking is that she has enjoyed a Sun-Venus conjunction in the summer of 1976, just when rumours were at their height, so it could truly be love, as far as she's concerned. All the same, not an obviously 'royal' horoscope.

There is no question of an arranged marriage. Charles will be free to marry whom he likes, even though his mother's permission, as monarch, is required before the wedding can go ahead. The exact Venus–Pluto sextile in his birth-chart indicates that he has a 'destined' love life. He will be drawn towards the right girl and will fall deeply, committedly, in love.

The one snag is his Venus–Neptune conjunction. This makes Charles a perfectionist in romance. He has a wealth of idealism to bring to his marriage, but it's surprising how easily he can feel hurt and betrayed. There is always the danger of being disillusioned in love. Charles must know this – and that's why he is taking his time in picking the right girl.

Andrew and Edward

If Prince Charles fails to marry, or marries and has no children, or simply drops down dead, we shall have our first-ever King Andrew. He is still a teenage schoolboy at Gordonstoun and has not yet emerged as an individual on the public stage, but astrology shows that he is perhaps the most fascinating and interesting of the younger Royals.

Like his elder brother Charles, Prince Andrew has Leo rising, but there are two important differences in their birth-charts which affect the way in which these Leonian characteristics manifest themselves in their personalities. Andrew was born on 19 February 1960 at 3.30 p.m., which means that the rebellious planet Uranus was in the crucial First House, just below the eastern horizon. This makes Andrew much more of a conscious individualist than Charles will ever be. Andrew needs to be *different*; he will not be happy unless he can show the world what the *real* Prince Andrew is like. To do this, he will need to turn his back on some aspects of his upbringing, and there are two ways in which this could be done. It's possible, as he moves through adolescence, that he will be politically interested in radical ideas that encourage him to reject the Royal Family as an out-dated anachronism. In his case, being different might involve becoming ordinary, like the man in the street. The other possibility, rather more likely, is that he will establish his individuality in a somewhat gaudy, theatrical, outlandish manner, for he is, after all, a Leo-rising person. My own hunch is that he will take a rather glamorous, romantic attitude towards his title as Prince, and hark back – in his own mind, at least – to the bigger-than-life nobility of the past as an inspiration to his own conduct. He is likely to be an outward-going character.

I said there were two differences between Leo Charles and Leo

Andrew. In Charles's case, you will recall, the Sun (ruler of Leo) lies in the Fourth House to do with home and family influence. In Andrew's chart, it's in the much more gregarious, outward-looking Seventh House to do with other people. Andrew's great desire will be to please others – not necessarily by doing his duty, or carrying out orders, or changing his personality to suit the requirements of others, but simply because he wants to be pleasant, popular and considered a nice chap.

He is much more of an extrovert than Charles. His birth-chart zings with a kind of show-business charisma that should make him a successful and appreciated figure in public life. In a few years' time, newspapers will thank their lucky stars – well, Andrew's lucky stars, actually – that he is providing such wonderful copy for the next editions. Andrew will be very publicity-conscious. He will want to get *his* views across to the public. He will enjoy leading the Press a merry dance at times, but he will also use it constructively at times to gain access to public opinion.

The trouble with Andrew is that he may not know quite what he wants to do. For although he will certainly be full of great plans, he may lack the expertise and stamina to put them into effect. This is true of anyone with the Sun in the Seventh House; they get a bit dithery or can lose heart half-way through. This is particularly true of Prince Andrew, for the Zodiac sign in which his Sun lies is the most wispy and indecisive of them all: Pisces the fish.

Think of an iridescent fish, all swerves and curls in its oceanic world, a creature responding to the least pressure and current, seemingly free, seemingly aimless, a tender thing, vulnerable if caught but swift to evade capture in the first place. This is the Piscean character – a bit magical and out-of-this-world, very tender, very escapist. Prince Andrew has access to the inner worlds of imagination and sympathy. He is an artist at heart, and his highest ambition will probably be to translate a private vision into a real, solid, public declaration: perhaps a play, a painting, a piece of music, or, most likely of all, photographs and movies. There is something in Andrew's chart that smacks of the cinema. I am sure he already loves to lose himself in the fantasy world of films. I am sure, too, that he will want to make films himself when

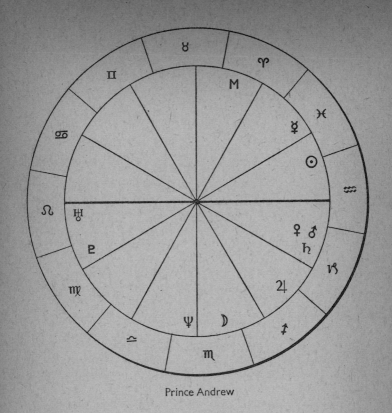

Prince Andrew

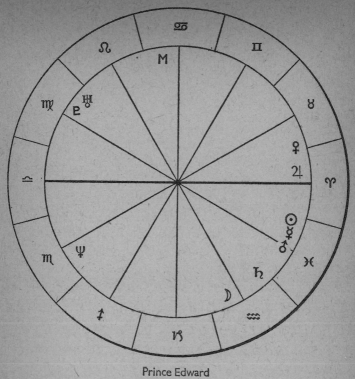

Prince Edward

he is older. He may start with nature films, but will want to be involved with proper feature-length motion pictures at some stage in his life.

He has a Sun–Pluto opposition, suggesting that he knows he has a special destiny to fulfil . . . but doesn't know at once what it will be. He may well get stuck in the wrong job, to start with – the Navy, for instance. I suppose every royal male must have some experience of the armed forces, and Andrew is drawn to both the sea and the air, but he is not an aggressive type nor the clannish type who enjoys all-male society. He will be twenty-four years old before he realizes where his true vocation lies.

It's possible that he has a special royal destiny as well. The last two crowned kings of England were both second sons whose elder brothers failed to attain – or keep – the Crown. The big upset in the Royal Family indicated in the early 1990s affects Andrew, too, for his Moon in Scorpio falls in this same fateful third decanate which is so significant in the charts of George VI, Elizabeth and Charles.

One thing is certain: Prince Andrew will grow into an attractive young man indeed. The two planets involved, Mars and Venus, lie exactly side by side, and this conjunction neatly bisects the angle between his Sun and Jupiter. He will act as a magnet to young women – not simply because of his royal connections but due to his strong personal charisma. In turn, he will be susceptible to their charm and flattery, and is more likely to lead a lively bachelor existence than his more rigorous, dutiful brother Charles. Besides, they inhabit different generations, for Charles is twelve years the elder. Andrew's influential years will be the 1980s, when a new spiritual awareness will colour his outlook: something far removed from the simple pieties of the Anglican faith. I would not be surprised if Andrew became a devotee of a worldwide movement. He is too independent by nature to commit himself whole-heartedly to any organization – be it a religious sect or the Royal Family itself – but he will be drawn to a set of ideas based on spiritual *science*.

His younger brother Edward, the baby of the family, is also a Piscean, and, like Andrew, has his ruler in the soft, easy-going

Seventh House. These two boys seem slightly apart from their older siblings and parents, and it may be that together they will introduce a fresh, invigorating note into the Royal Family.

But, whereas Andrew has the strong, sunny Leo as his rising sign, Edward has Libra for an Ascendant, the same as his grandfather George VI. This, combined with a Piscean Sun, makes him an exceptionally gentle sort of boy, always seeking harmony and peace and never really *wanting* to stir up trouble. He has a well-mannered disposition, and in some ways he is more an onlooker than a participant, a referee rather than a player.

At worst, he could develop into an easily led individual, serving others without knowing what he really wants for himself. Certainly he is not a showy person, out to grab attention. He is very sensitive, and can easily be hurt by a thoughtless word or action.

What saves him from too much soppiness is a triple Sun–Mercury–Mars conjunction. Although he may not *want* to cause a fuss, he cannot always help himself. Inwardly he will boil up in rages, and then not know what to do with his frustration and anger, for by training and character he is not encouraged to be too open with his feelings. I can imagine Edward being bullied by other boys and not wanting to fight back; or full of passion but not being able to express himself; or bottling up his emotions because they are unsuitable in polite company. Then, alone and in private, he'll explode!

I imagine he has a sharp, critical mind, and it would not surprise me if he decided to read Law at university. As a member of the Royal Family he may not be able to practise at the Bar, but he could become a constitutional lawyer at the Foreign Office.

If he is not clever enough, he will express this interest in legal matters simply at a fantasy level (watching TV detective series, reading thrillers) and probably enter the Navy, like many of his relatives before him. All those planets in fishy Pisces, plus a pleasant trine to the planet of the sea, Neptune, in the sailor's sign of Scorpio, marks young Edward as a natural mariner.

He has also a poetic imagination. Andrew will need to show his artistic talents to the world, but Edward will be more circumspect and private. I can see him dashing off impetuous love letters to someone close to his heart, but not wanting to publish his works to the public gaze!

Love and marriage will be crucial to Edward's happiness. He may not be as highly sexed as his brother Andrew, but is much more swooning and romantic. The two beneficial planets, Venus and Jupiter, lie in his Seventh House to do with close relationships, and he will be blessed with a lovely, soft, easy charm as far as women are concerned. Every youngest child tends to be spoilt, and this frequently spills over in his adult attitude towards romance. Edward will enjoy being pampered and fussed. He will probably be a pretty young man himself, and will want to be surrounded by pretty girlfriends, a pretty wife, good-looking children, all in happy, sweet, tasteful surroundings. I can imagine him reviving his grandfather's love of landscape gardening, if he gets the chance – and money – to do so.

Although Edward is eminently the marrying type, I think he will prolong his bachelor days until his late twenties.

In later years, his health may give cause for concern. I do not mean that he has a sickly constitution, but he could suffer from a disability that could be mildly irritating for the rest of his life. Increasing deafness is one possibility.

Anne and Mark

Her Royal Highness Princess Anne, horsewoman, glamour-girl and only daughter of the Queen, hits the headlines wherever she goes. She seems such a permanent fixture in the British social scene that it's hard to recall that only eight or nine years have elapsed since she left Benenden School as a lumpy, jodhpur-clad teenager. The sad fact is that she has only a handful of years left when she can be front-page news. At the moment, she is Royal Glamour Girl No. One, with only fractional competition from her first cousin Princess Alexandra. But soon there will be a new Princess of Wales. Then Andrew will marry. Then there will be a string of little princes and princesses, children of Charles and Andrew and, later, Edward, that will jump the queue in the line of accession to the throne and elbow Anne into the shadows.

This makes grim reading for a girl who loves the gentle adulation of the crowds. Oh, she has played games with the Press and torn strips off intrusive photographers in her time, but on the whole she enjoys their generous blandishments. Naturally she will continue a number of royal duties, but as the Family expands with the introduction of young new offspring, Anne must be content with retirement into semi-private life.

The truth is that Anne is a determined, headstrong girl who needs a positive outlet for her talents. Her strength comes from two sources: Mars rising, and a Sun–Pluto conjunction in the Tenth House.

Most people would agree that Anne combines a good deal of charm with a fairly blunt, forthright approach to life. This mixture of feminine grace and masculine energy can be traced back to the sky rising above the eastern horizon at 10.50 on the morning of 15 August 1950. Her Ascendant is the sweet sign of Libra, but her

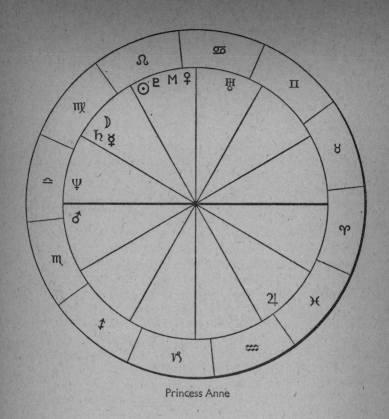

Princess Anne

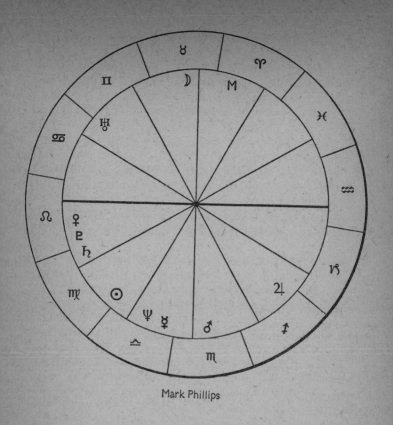

Mark Phillips

rising planet situated in the First House is quite the opposite influence: fiery Mars.

It's fascinating to recall that her grandfather had Libra rising, too, but the soft, gentle planet Venus in the First House. This explains his retiring nature. Anne is much more of the tomboy. Certainly she is well-mannered and agreeable, as you would expect from a Libran Ascendant, but this graciousness is set afire all too often by the rough, tough, decisive planet Mars. She is a wolf in sheep's clothing.

Mars is the god of battle in ancient mythology, and Anne's is a battling temperament. She does not accept defeat or failure in her own heart, however much a good loser she may appear as a sportswoman. She is competitive and eager to succeed. If she is beaten, her instinct is to pause for breath and then wade into the fray again!

The natural demeanour of anyone with Mars rising is aggressive. In Anne's case, her bluntness is softened by her Libran Ascendant, just as a searchlight beam can be diffused by misty air, but it's still visible. It makes her over-hasty in her judgements. It encourages a real love of outdoors sports. And it makes her a commanding young woman, wanting to get her own way. I imagine she truly enjoys wearing military uniform. She is a soldier at heart.

If Charles's horoscope seems to resemble his mother's, then Anne has a great deal in common with her father. Philip, remember, has a close Sun–Mars conjunction to equal the force of Anne's Mars in the First House. And both of them are Fire–Air people, with Ascendant and Sun-sign in either Fire or Air. These two elements feed off each other; they are both anti-gravitational and a bit ethereal, compared with the heaviness and 'realness' of Earth or Water. Air–Fire people are spitfires. And Anne, with her Sun in Leo, is no exception.

One glance at her stance, the cock of her head, the style of her hair, reveals her as a true Leonian. She loves to sweep her blonde lion's mane back from her broad forehead and around her face, like the corona round the Sun itself. The generous brow-line, the cheek bones, the full mouth, the proud jaw – these are the sure signs of the Leo girl. There is no pussy-cat mincing here; this is the king of the beasts. She needs her place in the sun where she can sprawl in graceful ease. So long as she is loved, honoured and respected, she is happy enough.

All Leonians are basically simple people. By 'simple' I do not mean 'plain', for Leo people enjoy luxury where possible. But they avoid complex, neurotic, detailed, penny-pinching attitudes. Their whole approach to life is on a broad, generous scale. At its best, this Leo quality leads to a lovely fresh ingenuous attitude where life is a series of enthusiasms one after the other. Anne can radiate pleasure in this honest, open, child-like way. It is one of the most attractive qualities in her character.

But she is not content to use her Leonian attributes in a purely passive manner. It was mid-morning when she was born, with the Sun hanging up there in the Tenth House at its most glorious and vivid. She is a career girl at heart, someone who needs to impress her talents on the community – quite the opposite, indeed, to her brother Charles, whose Sun in the Fourth House, on the other side of the Earth, makes him a more introspective, absorbing sort of individual.

The other source of her strength is the Sun–Pluto conjunction in this Tenth House. Normally a Libran Ascendant can make a person pretty indecisive, caught between choices and unable to pick the appropriate course of action. In little everyday ways, Anne will er and um at times – and then make up her mind with a sharp burst of Martian energy! But in important matters, especially those to do with her 'career', she can be quite obsessive in her concentration and stamina. Pluto always adds *seriousness* to the parts of the horoscope which it touches. Once she gets her teeth into an activity she likes – and her principal interest seems to be show-jumping – she can devote long hours of practice and preparation and during the event itself conjure up that extra ounce of will-power which can make all the difference between winning and losing.

If, as I believe, Princess Anne takes up a professional career as horse trainer, she will throw deep reserves of energy and resourcefulness into the enterprise. She has luck on her side.

She has a few problems as well. There is an interesting Moon–Mercury–Saturn conjunction in Virgo which works as a disadvantage in her early years but will become another source of strength as she moves into middle age. A Moon–Saturn contact like this produces an element of strain in the relationship with her mother. Anne and Queen Elizabeth do not have a great deal in common. The older woman is a more rigorous, disciplined character, while the younger one is more free-wheeling and impulsive. They never give the impression of being desperately close to each other, in the way that clearly Anne and Philip do. But it's wrong to 'blame' the Queen for this state of affairs. With a Moon–Saturn conjunction in her chart, Anne is 'meant' to be independent of the Mother archetype from an early age, even though at times, perhaps for no obvious reason, she has felt excluded from her mother's affections. This, in turn, will pass on to Anne's own role as mother. I doubt whether Anne yearns to be a cuddly, breast-feeding mum; Saturn so close to her Moon makes her apprehensive about her ability as a mother, and possibly she has deliberately avoided having a child quickly after her marriage for this very reason.

It's interesting to note, by the way, how the Queen's own Saturn is fixed like the key-stone of her family circle. It forms an awkward square to Prince Philip's Moon ('emotional reserve' by her towards him at times); a conjunction to Charles's Sun and Andrew's Moon (ditto); and a square to Anne's Sun (ditto again). Emotionally this marks her as a person apart; constitutionally it shows how her sense of discipline and duty holds the family together, at whatever cost to their personal relationships.

Charles's Saturn does not perform the same task within the horoscopes of his brothers and sister. When he comes to the Throne, he may not be able to maintain the same unity and cohesion that the present monarch commands.

The announcement that Princess Anne would marry Captain Mark Phillips took everyone but astrologers by surprise. Since the Sun was twenty-two degrees away from the Moon in her birth-chart, she was likely to 'come into her own' in her twenty-second year; and since Venus was twenty-three degrees away from the Sun, it was likely to be a romantic fulfilment. Sure enough, they fell in love in 1972, and the following year they were wed.

The other surprise, to people who knew a little astrology, was that the big, bouncy Leo girl was going to marry a reticent *Virgo* type! But once you examine their horoscopes in greater depth, you find some remarkable points of rapport.

Mark was born on 22 September 1948 'at about two o'clock in the morning', his mother tells me. Straightaway this brings him within the Princess Anne ambit, for it gives him a Leo Ascendant quite close to her own Leo Midheaven. Two lions together can be too much of a good thing, but equally they share many interests and outlook. They both like being bolstered up by flattery and attention, and their strong pride can be an obstacle to harmony, for it is hard for either of them to give way and admit a mistake.

The interesting difference, especially bearing in mind the Princess's links with her grandfather George VI, is that Mark has the soft and agreeable planet Venus in the First House, just like George. So Anne is the bossy Martian type, while Mark is the soothing Venusian counterpart.

This means she will get her own way in a great many matters, for her instinct is to fight for victory while his is to maintain peace and harmony within the relationship.

Now we come to the Sun in Virgo. The Virgoan character is a neat, painstaking one. The main motivation is the need to be efficient, and the principal means used to achieve this is a sharp critical attitude, throwing out the unwanted and retaining only the worthwhile. We have seen how such an attitude led to a mean, carping nature in the Prince Consort, back in Victoria's day. In Mark's case, the Sun is only just still in Virgo, for it occupies the final twenty-ninth degree and is on the point of moving into the gentle, charming sign of Libra. So he's 'on the cusp', half-way between the Virgo and Libran temperaments, and in these circumstances you can sense them uneasily merging and separating. The individual is often caught between two identities and may never quite know who he is or where his true directions lie. An example that comes to mind is the writer and singer George Melly, who has the same twenty-ninth degree of Virgo as his Ascendant. George spends half his life as a Virgo critic and half as a Libran musician.

In his own way, it will be the same with Mark Phillips. One part of him wants to be the cleancut, no-nonsense Virgo Army technocrat, and the other half is probably more artistic and a bit self-indulgent and vaguely wanting a pleasant country existence.

His Sun lies in the Second House, so he's interested in money. Yes, he's married well, but that won't be quite enough; he'll want to *earn* cash, and the life of the gentleman farmer-cum-stud-breeder could be his means of making a profit out of life.

Anne's Sun, remember, lies in the Tenth House of the career, which is exactly where Mark's Moon lies. (Her Moon's in Virgo, where his Sun is, so there are lots of under-the-surface links between these two.) Mark's Moon in this position resembles that of the dear old Prince of Wales, Bertie. Bertie was a great success with women, and Mark has the same aptitude. Of course he's not a professional womanizer, but dressed in his Hussars uniform with the peak of his cap pulled *just so* above that sharp, sweet angular profile – oh yes, Mark knows all about being charming. He should take a job where this charm can be put to good use – dealing with clients or customers, sympathizing with them, teaching them, making himself agreeable.

Anne's Moon, as we have seen, is somewhat curtailed and frustrated by Saturn. For all her Leonian warmth and ardour, she will have her cold moods. It's all very well being self-controlled on public occasions, but there are private moments when such coolness can only be a hindrance. My guess is that Mark will take over some roles as 'mother' of the household with complete ease and assurance. He will enjoy working at home, looking after the kids fairly often, helping in the kitchen, while Anne is away on an official duty.

What sort of a future do they have together? Mark has an exact Venus–Pluto conjunction in his chart, meaning that he has a totally 'fated' destiny as far as his love life is concerned. He will have been drawn willy-nilly into his marriage, magnetized by the force of the attraction between them and the irresistible force of circumstances. But this kind of Venus–Pluto contact is a mixed blessing. Just as it can draw you inseparably together, so it can make any parting all the more painful and tragic. It's known as the divorce-type aspect because so often it leads the person concerned up the primrose path into an emotional cul-de-sac from which there is no obvious escape. Mark could well have recently emerged from an unhappy and failed love affair in 1970–71, shortly before he met and fell in love with Anne. A similar planetary aspect comes in 1988–9, which are years that are bound to be crucial in Mark's love life in some way. Mark's fortieth year is a time when he may need to come to terms with a crisis in his life: it may be a difficult turning-point in his relationship with Anne.

Anne has nothing similar in her own chart, which makes me think that the relationship concerned will not involve Anne at all, even if she knows about it. Hers is a bonny disposition, sexually as well as in her normal everyday demeanour. The Venus–Mars square in her chart denotes a strong libido, with a powerful impetus towards jealousy if she is ever given cause.

The early years of any marriage reveal little about the true rapport – or conflicts – that will emerge later. Time is needed for the trivial little tensions to disappear and the real incompatibilities, if any, to develop. If a composite birth-chart is made of their two horoscopes, with the Ascendant formed by finding the midway point between Anne's Ascendant and Mark's Ascendant, and so forth with every planet, you discover an interesting situation. Their midway Ascendant forms a close conjunction with their midway Sun and midway Saturn. This suggests a tremendous binding together of their innermost personalities. Saturn can be a gaoler. Anne and Mark are chained together, sometimes with happiness, sometimes with pain and problems. There is bound to be a power struggle between them, for Mark cannot surrender all the time. There are bound to be silence and secret thoughts, especially if they ever encounter failure together – in their business life, perhaps.

At worst, these difficulties will force them apart. At best, these two lions will realize that life is not simply a bask in the equatorial Sun, and through setback and disappointments they will find the real love that imprisons them in joy.

The Snowdons

Every generation has its black sheep, and the Royal Family is no exception. Bertie, Alfie, David – and now Margaret – have all been cast as villains in the popular imagination, thereby living out the age-old need of humankind to throw mud at those set up in authority and prestige over them.

In each case, the royal figure has seemed to 'go too far' and break certain unwritten codes of etiquette. When this happens, there has usually been a split between the Establishment and the ordinary people of England about the rights and wrongs of the situation. Bertie offended Court circles and the Victorian middle classes by his loose living, but the working classes were usually on his side. David, too, offended a constitutional point of principle about which the Government, Church and high-minded people felt very strongly indeed; but many average young people, filled with democratic virtue, claimed that he should be able to marry whom he chose and still remain on the Throne.

Princess Margaret has been neither a particularly loose liver nor a breaker of constitutional verities, yet in many people's minds she is cast as the 'Naughty Sister'. A proper little madam, too pompous, too privileged, living off the State, taking too many holidays abroad – these are the sort of comments linked with this aspect of the Margaret Myth. But there's another aspect too, this time the Wistful Captive. She's not really happy, she's never got over Peter Townsend, she'll never be truly fulfilled, say the adherents of this particular faith. Many of them, I dare say, enjoy historical romances, and some of them have declared that our own dear Margaret Rose is a reincarnation of Mary, Queen of Scots, while her sister Elizabeth II is the soul of Elizabeth I returned to earth again. Hence the rivalry, the jealousies between them. Narrow, upright Protestant Elizabeth has triumphed yet again over the generous-hearted, warmer, Catholic Mary-Margaret.

I do not sneer at reincarnation – indeed, I am sure that we all do spend many seasons on earth, blooming for a brief summer, dying back, and flowering again. But the process is far more complex and disguised than is usually believed, and what does return – the 'soul' – is far more rarefied and abstract than the part of a human being which we normally recognize as a personality – namely the 'ego', which does indeed die like petals when the frosts appear.

For the life of me, there seems precious little resemblance between the two Elizabeths, for the Virgin Queen was a cold, scheming Virgo while our own Queen is a very apolitical, Ideal Family Taurean. There are even fewer similarities between Mary and Margaret, though their looks are remarkably alike; for Mary was a well-meaning, idealistic Piscean, while Margaret is another of these modern royal lionesses. There are so many of them that every time I see a notice to the Windsor Safari Park, I assume they mean the Castle.

Margaret was born on 21 August 1930, at Glamis Castle, at 8.22 p.m. She has Aries rising, like her grandfather George V, and like him she has a quick, sharp temper. But whereas he would explode with rage when his conventional life was upset, Margaret uses her anger to stir things up. She likes to be unpredictable. She keeps guests on their toes, and wants to surround herself with interesting, out-of-the-ordinary people. For, like her young nephew Andrew, she has the disruptive planet Uranus in the First House. She hates life to be too placid and boring.

So she is quite different from her sister Elizabeth. Lilibet (as she is known in the family) is a very Earthy type, while Margaret is ablaze with Fire, with Aries and Leo as her Ascendant and Sun-sign respectively. As Crawfie, their governess when they were children, remarked about Margaret: 'She was warm and demonstrative . . . her father would be almost embarrassed, yet at the same time most touched and pleased, when she wound her arms round his neck, nestled against him and cuddled and caressed him.' Lilibet was the shy, self-controlled one. That's the difference between Fire and Earth.

Margaret grew up as a bright, highly-strung, impressionable girl,

137

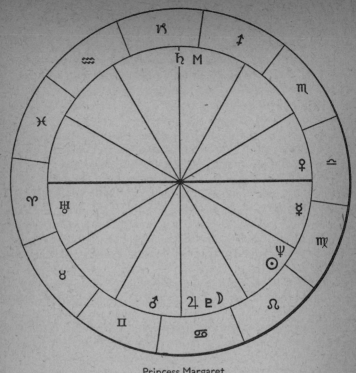

Princess Margaret

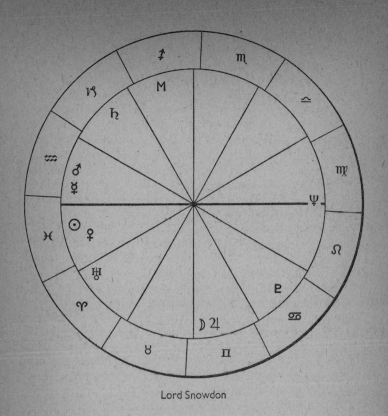

Lord Snowdon

very precocious, sometimes the little minx with older men, certainly capable of mimicking others, seeing the ludicrous in everything, and reducing the company to utter laughter when she was in the mood. 'She is so outrageously amusing,' old Queen Mary once said, 'that one can't help encouraging her.' Partly this stemmed from the wonderfully mischievous Uranus rising, partly from her natural Leonian desire to be a show-off.

Margaret has always loved the theatre itself and the night-club life where everyone concerned – stars, celebrities, even the waiters – become actors in an evening of delight. Not only is she a Leo girl; her Sun lies in the Fifth House, to do with the recreational side of life, so it is natural for her to think of her existence as a perpetual holiday. Life, to Margaret, is meant to be enjoyed.

Although she is plainly cut out to lead a gay, high-spirited lifestyle, there is one factor holding her firmly in place. Like her sister the Queen, she has the planet of discipline, Saturn, placed on her Midheaven, signifying her career and destiny. Both of them, in other words, have a heavy responsibility to bear in terms of public life. Both of them wish, at times, that this load could be shifted from their shoulders; and both of them – as far as work is concerned – have an exaggerated respect for tradition. The Queen accepts the royal drudgery with more grace and earnestness than her live-wire younger sister, for she is a born businesswoman or civil servant. Margaret, the born actress, likes the fun and games that go with the job, but regrets the limitations imposed on her.

Even so, it's a mistake to assume that Margaret is solely a frivolous woman. She has Saturn built into her psychological make-up, and can be a serious, caring woman in a crisis. Remarking on his portrait of Princess Margaret, the painter Pietro Annigoni said: 'The rigid left arm, draped and unseen, represents her unshakeable strength; the right arm her volatility and impulsiveness.' He might almost have been talking about Saturn and Uranus, the two most important planets in her life.

They both played an important role in Margaret's romantic crisis, which lasted for four years of increasing doubt, defiance and devotion. She was torn between independence (Uranus) and duty (Saturn), and in the end it was Saturn which won.

The King's Equerry, Peter Townsend, had been in and out of the palace since the war years, when he had distinguished himself as a fighter pilot. He was a man of courage and good humour and undoubted integrity. His one blemish, as it might be seen in those days, was his marriage, which had broken down through no fault of his own; but the King found him such a good chap that he refused to let Townsend resign when his divorce became imminent.

It is always claimed that Margaret and Peter grew close to each other soon after the King died in early 1952. I believe that Margaret was first attracted to him before then, in the previous autumn, when the planet Jupiter was transiting her First House (always a time of joy and personal fulfilment) and Uranus formed a transit square to Venus. These two planets are directly opposite each other in her horoscope, marking her as a woman of sudden, unexpected passion in a direction that people would find surprising. This love of the bizarre has followed Margaret throughout her life, but this was the first time that it was strongly at work in her chart.

Her grief at losing her beloved father coincided with the comfort she found in Peter, a man sixteen years her senior. By the following year, relatives and palace staff were beginning to notice how much time the couple were spending together. It was clearly a sexual attraction, as his vivid Mars–Venus conjunction formed a beautiful trine to her Ascendant. Peter was born on 22 November 1914, making him, like Mark Phillips, a cuspal baby caught between Scorpio and Sagittarius. The Sun's position triggered the exact mid-point of Margaret's Venus and Pluto, signifying her obsessive love nature. She became hooked on him, but equally significant, he was head over heels in love with her and urged her to marry him.

Here a legal problem intruded. The new Queen had to give her permission to any marriage contracted by Margaret, and as the Head of the Church of England she could hardly approve a match with a man who was divorced and whose former wife was still alive. It was precisely the same situation as David and Wallis, twenty years earlier. The monarchy could not change its attitude in the space of one generation.

But there was one loophole. When Princess Margaret became twenty-five, in two years' time, she would be free of the Queen's control – free to marry the man she loved. It was simply a question of waiting.

Peter was transferred to Brussels, and for family, friends and, by this stage, Press and public, it became a long-drawn-out game of 'Will she, won't she?' At some times (August 1954, January 1955, June 1955) she was under strong Uranian influence to do her own thing and sacrifice her position as third in line to the Throne. Neptune, too, was adding fuel to the flames of escape, freedom . . . and fantasy.

The crunch came in the autumn of 1955. Throughout October, the planet Uranus formed a close, crucial aspect to her Midheaven, just as it had in uncle David's chart when he chose freedom back in 1936. To that extent, she was pressured towards breaking free from public duty. But deeper, more ineluctable forces were at work in her psyche. The planet Saturn, representing sacrifice, was moving opposite Pluto, representing her obsession with Peter Townsend. The planet Neptune, too, formed a gentle and helpful aspect to her Sun, indicating that the religious and conscientious side of the problem was weighing heavily in her mind. Finally, and most important of all, the planet Pluto moved exactly conjunct her Sun on 13 October, signifying the ultimate turning-point of her life, with one phase of life ending and a new one beginning. This was the day when she met Peter for the first time in eighteen months, and the day she must have decided that they had no future together. 'I would like it to be known', she announced on 31 October, 'that I have decided not to marry Group Captain Peter Townsend.' As if to sweeten the pill, Jupiter formed a conjunction with the Sun on that day. She must have heaved a sigh of relief. She was free of her dilemma.

A little over three years later, she was to find the man of her choice. Tony Armstrong-Jones, a double Piscean, was a very different kettle of fish to the Scorpian Peter Townsend, and there is little point in comparing them. A woman's heart can be fixed for a number of years on a particular type of man – then abruptly discover that she wanted something else all the time.

In Tony she found a steadfast chameleon, a man of subtle innocence who was disarmingly secretive, full of charm and gaiety with a steely inner core of seriousness.

He was born on 7 March 1930, in London, at, it's believed, 6.15 a.m., though no one is quite sure. This makes him a double Piscean, with the Ascendant and Sun in this sign, exactly the opposite of dear Albert, the Prince Consort, who had the Sun and Ascendant in the opposing sign of Virgo. And what a difference! Think of Albert as a stiff, cold, unfeeling man who did everything by the rulebook; and think of Tony the artist, affable and sensitive, human to the *nth* degree.

Anyone with the Sun rising in Pisces is essentially a private person driven to express himself in public. (Another example springing to mind, besides Tony, is the actor Tom Courtenay.) The Piscean temperament is elusive and inward-turning; it absorbs rather than projects; and it dislikes being pinned down or forced to make a decision. The fish, the fluttering moth, the ebb and flow and eddy of sea-water among rocks are all natural images that briefly capture the Piscean mood: ever-changing, living half in fantasy and half in the real world, too delicate to survive for long in the rough and tumble of life, it would seem. But survive they do, however beaten they may become; for fish themselves, as well as the sea they live in, are flexible things, surviving through adaptation to the least pressure.

Against this malleable, quivering sort of outer temperament must be set the rising Sun, symbol of power and energy and radiance. This is the contradiction in Tony's character. In one way, he is a retiring individual, in another a dominant, self-confident person with a great deal to offer the world.

The immature way of dealing with this character would be for the sensitive, even masochistic element to hold too great a sway, preventing the solar power from properly fulfilling itself. The fictional hero Billy Liar is just such a creature, wanting power and prestige but never putting his fantasies into action. The mature way is beautifully illustrated by Tony Snowdon himself; the delicate, shifting, restless Piscean temperament is held under firm control by the purposeful Sun in the First House. I am sure it has taken him many years to attain this maturity, and in his youth he may well have dithered about decisions and left jobs half-completed.

I must say that I have slight doubts about his Piscean Ascendant.

Suppose he was born at 6.10 a.m., just five minutes earlier than stated. This would put his Ascendant straddling across the tail-end of Aquarius and the start of Pisces, so that he would exhibit both signs simultaneously in his outer temperament. Think of that cool, rational manner of his, the independence of outlook, the soft determination to be truthful. Think of his aviary at London Zoo, a gossamer cage for the creatures of the air. Think of his profession, photography and television, which are such Aquarian pursuits. I believe he was born with the twenty-ninth degree of Aquarius rising, still making Pisces a crucial element in his psychological make-up but providing that lightness, that curiosity, that sharp observation of life which is such a marked characteristic of his. It would put Princess Margaret's Sun directly on his Seventh House cusp, to do with her marriage. It couldn't be more appropriate.

For years before their separation, the European Press claimed all sorts of weird goings-on between Tony and Margaret; that they weren't getting on with each other, they were on the point of divorce, they went their separate ways. Clearly there was an element of truth in some of this, for they are certainly different people. Margaret is volatile. She was first attracted to Tony because he was *different*; his Uranus, indeed, representing his unconventionality, lies very close to her Ascendant, so once their *minds* clicked, there would be magic between them. And theirs was far more a mental relationship than a purely physical one. Margaret herself has an exact square aspect between Mercury (talking) and Mars (anger), so she is sharp-tempered at times but in fact revels in a good scintillating argument. It's similar with Tony; he has the same planets in a close conjunction, and this conjunction, in turn, forms a close contact with Margaret's Mercury–Mars aspect. At times, the words flow like blows, and while Margaret is the more aggressive of the two, Tony has the strength to look after himself.

Certainly they led independent lives, partly by choice, partly through the demands of their different jobs. In the last years of their marriage, Tony accompanied Margaret increasingly less on official functions, and naturally she did not go with him on his photographic assignments, which may take him to the grim backstreets of an American ghetto area or the parched spaces of the Australian desert. What they did share in common was a love of domestic life. Both have the Moon in the Fourth House, to do with home and family, so both crave the peace that comes from happy days among their own surroundings with their own growing children.

Why did the marriage fail? Tony has Neptune on his Seventh House cusp, so clearly his marriage, begun in high hopes, eventually proved disillusioning. But he was no fortune-hunter back in 1959–60, when the pair fell in love and married. At this time, Mars had moved by direction to conjoin his planet of love Venus, so at a sexy, romantic level Tony was deeply involved with Margaret. In turn, she enjoyed a beautiful Venus–Jupiter trine in 1959 and a warm, sensual Mars–Moon conjunction in 1960.

One difficulty in the marriage stemmed from Margaret's undoubted propensity to be snobbish and pompous at times. If she isn't treated as a Leo princess, she cuts you dead. Tony, especially with an Aquarian Ascendant, cannot abide snobbery of any kind, though equally he will have no time for phonies and sycophants. Equally, Margaret felt that Tony didn't get *involved* enough in everyday life. If you spend your days behind a glass lens, so to speak, you do resemble a fish in a bowl, forever seeing life at a distance, objectively, without being an actor yourself.

And Margaret does have this incredibly frisky Venus–Jupiter–Uranus configuration, providing her with a zest for sudden friendships, like a glass of champagne on a chilly day. If you object that the girl who renounced love at the age of twenty-five could hardly become a woman of the world twenty years later, I suggest that you do not know much about human nature. Her birth-chart shows that at certain times (winter 1970–71, late summer 1971) she has been under strong inner pressure to throw caution to the winds, and that at the present time (right through 1977) the presence of Pluto conjoining her Venus is marking some kind of make-or-break experience in her life; not only the dissolution of her marriage, but perhaps a deep, searing other relationship as well.

I am sad that Tony and Margaret's marriage had to break up. It could still have provided plenty of stimulation for them both. Every Leonian, like Margaret, wants to be loyal, provided she receives enough attention. Every Piscean, like Tony, wants to be trusting, provided his faith is not shattered. I don't think either of them ever did anything secret, without the knowledge of the other partner.

My other sadness is that Princess Margaret has not fulfilled the creative side of her nature. It may be that the rigorous royal training in her early years stamped out the idea that she could ever perform in public. It may be that marriage to a professional artist – a complete perfectionist, in fact – has daunted her ambition to attempt anything at all. It may be, indeed, she has a common human condition: a creative temperament without the accompanying talents. Evidently her midnight efforts at the piano à la Ella Fitzgerald are rarely in key, but perhaps it's all malicious gossip.

Gossip has it, too, that Snowdon and Edinburgh could never abide each other. It's true that Philip's Saturn (coldness) lies midway between Tony's Sun and Venus, suggesting some inhibitions at first. They come from different backgrounds – minor royalty and the Navy, on the one hand, and louche artistic upper-middle-class and journalism, on the other. Tony cannot stand the barbaric royal penchant for murdering animals, and Philip may have had little patience with Tony in the early days when Tony was trying to be a working photographer *and* husband to the monarch's sister. It had never been done before, but in his quiet persistent way Tony got palace and people to accept that he could be 'royal' and 'commercial' without ever taking advantage of his position. In this respect, he has done more to give an acceptable modern image to the Royal Family than all the rest put together.

The Snowdons' children, Lord Lindley and Lady Sarah, have grown up in a relatively unfettered atmosphere, moving from private prep schools to the co-educational progressive school, Bedales, together. Young David bears a resemblance to old Bertie, King Edward VII, for both of them have birth-charts with Sagittarius rising, the Sun in Scorpio, Moon in Scorpio and Venus in Libra! I expect David to develop into a challenging young man, unafraid of danger and eager to live up to high standards – his own, not those that others may seek to impose on him. His is a strong, self-possessed horoscope. He should certainly be able to cope with life at an everyday level, but this gay, brave front may sometimes hide a much more worried, insecure interior consciousness. Scorpio, as we have seen, can be a tortured character, anxious about matters that the rest of us would not bother tuppence about. David will grow into a fairly extrovert Scorpian, but a Scorpian he'll be – intense, devoted, self-critical and, at times, bloody-minded.

He is a very 'giving' person. With Moon in the Ninth House of travel and Sun in the Eleventh House of friendships, he'll spend a lot of time on the move, meeting and mixing with a wide variety of folk. Although he has one very charming aspect, a conjunction between Mercury and Venus which he shares with his beloved grandmother the Queen Mother, he is not notably artistic. I see him as a practical scientist or manager, interested in real problems involving men, machines and resources. He could well have a talent for languages, chemistry and biology, and if he goes to university I expect him to read one of those subjects. But much depends on the school, together with those intangible royal dictates which may encourage him to pursue a line of studies more in keeping with any royal duties he will perform. Thus he might read Politics, Philosophy and Economics, or one of the General Studies courses at a newer university: Sussex, perhaps.

One aspect, a Mars–Saturn opposition, suggests that he may not find his feet all that quickly. It is much easier for a comparative unknown like Tony Armstrong-Jones to come down from Cambridge without a degree and learn to make his own living the hard way, than for Viscount Lindley, nephew to the Queen, to do so. This Mars–Saturn opposition falls exactly on the Queen's own Midheaven, suggesting that David may arouse the Queen's disapproval in some way. He may be intimidated by his royal connections, and 'fail' in his twenties as a result. The planet closest to his own Midheaven is the talkative, communicative Mercury, so I cannot help feeling that he will thrive in an institution such as the BBC, or a body linked to foreign affairs, where he can feel part of a group, spreading the word and keeping people in touch with the world. He has some interest in the Law, but he is more the conciliator than the ardent, probing advocate. Again, publishing would be an admirable profession for him to enter. Luckily, he's in a 'job' as member of the Royal Family where he can express some interest in all these activities: as honorary president of this or that, for instance.

He has two very vivid aspects denoting romance at the comparatively early age of twenty, so he will certainly be in love – and perhaps wanting to be married – quite soon. The lovely Mercury–Venus conjunction promises a happy marriage, with few complications.

If any teenage boy is looking for a nice, bright, happy and sympathetic wife, I suggest he looks no further than Lady Sarah Armstrong-Jones. She is a sweetie.

With Cancer rising, Sun in Taurus and Moon in Capricorn, she is a natural conservative, far more traditional in outlook than either of her parents. She is much more sane, balanced and secure than they. She has none of her mother's hair-raising spitfire qualities, nor her father's restless inner worries. She will settle for second-best, she will reach compromises, she will search – and find – the quiet, peaceful life.

Naturally, this will emerge later in life, from her twenties on. But already she will be her commonsensical good self. She has a lovely Sun–Mercury–Jupiter conjunction lifting those bovine Taurean spirits and giving her a pleasant, friendly, good-humoured demeanour. She'll do everything 'within reason'. By temperament she is the most motherly and cherishing of all the Royal Family. Provided she can find the right husband, she has the best hope of being 'happy' of all the people in this book.

She needs an education that will enable her to deal with real people, real problems, real opportunities. She needs to know how to tot up a balance sheet, how to make things work, how to organize a task into its constituent parts. Her ideal job, if she gets the chance, would be running a restaurant or hotel, or working in the fashion trade, or helping to run a crafts centre. But her real talent lies in marriage. She is not a Women's Libber by temperament, and will happily assume the supportive role towards the man she loves.

The Minor Royals

With the Gloucesters, the Kents and the Ogilvys we enter the realms of minor royalty. Cousin to the Queen is definitely not as grand as sister, son, daughter or even nephew. And besides, they are becoming two a penny. In recent years we have been starved of minor royalty. The previous monarch, George VI, had three brothers who could only muster five children between them. Our own Queen has only one sibling with a mere brace of offspring. But in a few years' time all the little princes and lords and earls and ladies will marry and bear children and in the 1980s and 1990s we shall be swamped with a Second XI and Third XI of Royals.

Relegation and promotion take place all the time, of course. Given a birth here, a death there, any member of the Royal Family can climb or drop a notch in the hierarchical ladder in as bewildering a fashion as members of the Soviet Politburo. Take the present Duke of Gloucester. When he was born as Prince Richard in 1944, he was fifth in line of the throne. Then his cousins Elizabeth and Margaret had six children between them, so he drops to eleventh position. But then, tragically, his elder brother William is killed flying his own aeroplane and soon afterwards his father dies, so he's up to ninth place again. But it can't last. Short of a mass assassination of the First XI at Parliament, Ascot or the Badminton Horse Trials, Richard will slip further and further from the chance of wearing the English Crown – and, to judge by his horoscope, he'll thank his lucky stars that he is never likely to hold such an unsuitable post.

Richard is not exactly an academic, but he is certainly the first *studious* member of the Royal Family since his great-great-grandfather the Prince Consort, and like him he's an out-and-out Virgo. Richard's birth-details (26 August 1944,

10.15 a.m.) give a horoscope with no less than half the solar system crammed into this one Zodiac sign. The Sun is there with Jupiter, Venus with Mercury, and Mars brings up the rear. No wonder, therefore, he is such a demure, inoffensive man. And while his ancestor Prince Albert showed the worst side of the Virgoan character, young Richard is an example of Virgo at its best. He tries not to nag or fret; he is peaceful in the extreme; and quiet goodness shines out of every pore in his soul.

He's helped by three factors in his birth-chart. First, he's got the gentle sign of Libra as his Ascendant, so he can't help being a jolly nice chap. Secondly, his ruler Venus is very close to Mercury, and as we've seen with the Queen Mum and several other relatives, this always leads to a mild, agreeable human politeness as well as an attractive sense of artistic taste.

Thirdly, Richard has a super Sun–Jupiter conjunction. If you can imagine a Virgo type being jovial, then the Duke of Gloucester is he. He likes to smile. Sun–Jupiter people can't stop smiling, in fact, because they are natural optimists and want to be friendly with everyone. They are also lucky. The Duke may not agree that he is a lucky man, for those two deaths in the family have meant that he's been practically forced to give up his profession of architecture in order to look after the ducal estates in Northamptonshire and carry out his share of official royal duties. (How interesting, by the way, and how uncommon it is, that in three generations the elder son of the family has died or abdicated, leaving his younger brother to take over the reins at a moment's notice.) But in the Duke's case, this sudden change in his career is indicated by the planet Pluto very close to his Midheaven ('a sense of destiny in his work'), and in his own manner and outlook he remains a pleasant, good-humoured man. Although architecture was an excellent choice for him – for Libra rising gives the artistic touch, while Sun in Virgo is excellent for the bricks-and-mortar side – his real destiny lies in those 'associations of peoples' with which the Eleventh House is linked. This is where Sun, Jupiter, Mercury and Venus lie, so whether this shy young man likes it or not, he will spend the bulk of his days visiting people, bringing them together, opening and celebrating and representing and performing all the other activities that make up the royal round.

Exactly what help the Duchess will be is an open question. He married this Danish-born former secretary in the days when he thought he would lead a quiet, private life as a government architect. She is a Geminian (born 20 June 1946) with the Moon in Pisces – an easy-going, thoroughly ordinary girl without a single distinctive factor in her horoscope. No one can doubt their love for each other; his Sun exactly conjoins her Mars (so he is the man in her life) while her Venus conjoins his Midheaven (her love and his destiny go hand in hand). But there is no evidence that a public way of life agrees with her. Like her husband, she will be glad whenever they can be alone together.

For two such mild and subfusc parents, Alexander, Earl of Ulster is an extraordinary child. He has half the solar system forming a conjunction in the tall-end of Libra and the beginning of Scorpio. And what a conjunction! The Sun, Mercury and Venus side by side with the fiery and explosive combination of Mars and Uranus! Little Alexander (he was born on 24 October 1974, prematurely, very early in the morning) will grow into a very interesting individual. There is a strong appetite for danger and excitement in his personality. I'm sure he will want to drive fast cars, go ski-ing and climb impossible mountains. He'll be a muscular but graceful man, very pleased with himself, wanting to exercise leadership and get his own way. He has a stubborn will, and his pride will get in the way of his commonsense at times. I should think he will enjoy service life, except that he is not good at taking orders from others. There's an inventive streak in his nature, and he'll enjoy pottering about with gadgets and being ingenious and resourceful in an emergency.

There are very close links with his father, whose own Ascendant lies slap-bang in the middle of Alexander's multiple conjunction. Father and son will be affectionate, angry, exasperated and tender towards each other. Mother will vainly try to keep order, but in the end will have to adapt herself to her strong-minded, wilful and talented son.

The other branch of the family is the Kent clan, a dukedom traditionally reserved for fourth sons of the monarch. The present Duke, known as Edward, is an amiable ex-Army officer married to a rather smashing blonde Yorkshire girl called Katharine. Edward has quite a crisp, curt outer temperament, wide-awake and critical, tidy-minded and efficient, stemming from his Virgo Ascendant. But, like his fellow-officer Mark Phillips, he has the agreeable planet Venus in the First House to make him a thoroughly pleasant fellow. (If you think that soldiers should have more aggressive horoscopes, you do not know the modern Army. Today's officers are models of courtesy and kindness, which suits the Duke, who is a Libran, down to the ground.) In fact, he is the most non-offensive man you could wish to meet, with his Moon in wishy-washy Pisces, and wishy-washy Neptune in his First House as well, and aggressive Mars playing a very low role in his horoscope altogether.

Perhaps this is the reason why he married a Piscean. His birthday was 9 October 1935, while hers was 22 February, two years earlier. It seems a bore to go on saying how nice and agreeable these members of the Royal Family are, but at least it's the truth according to their horoscopes. The Duchess, like so many of her royal contemporaries, has this Mercury–Venus conjunction which provides what may be called the *appreciative* temperament – that is, the ability to respond to beauty and politeness and good taste without being noticeably creative oneself. As usual, there are the appropriate compatibility links between their two charts. Her Sun lies on the cusp of his Seventh House of marriage (the ideal place, actually) while her Mars is somewhat sexily placed next to his Venus. Best of all, his Moon is incredibly close to her Sun in Pisces. I expect they dither a bit before making up their minds, and they may both be mild hypochondriacs worrying about possible ill-health. They won't argue much. They really are an ideal pair.

If the Duke ever consulted an astrologer, he wouldn't ask about his emotional life, which is happy and content, but about his financial position, which could be more precarious than people realize. He receives no money from the Government and his inherited wealth is probably small in comparison with other royal fortunes. His Sun in the Second House indicates that the most crucial choice facing him in life is how he should earn his money now he has left the Army. My hunch is that Angus Ogilvy will eventually come to the rescue, and Edward, Duke of Kent, will be the first royal prince to hold a directorship in the City of London.

Their three children form a nice contrast in human temperament. The eldest, George, the Earl of St Andrews, was born on 26 June 1962, at two o'clock in the afternoon. He is cast in essentially the same mould as his parents, with the 'soft' sign of Libra rising and the Moon in the Seventh House and the Sun in the 'mother's' sign of Cancer. George is a thoroughly good sort. He will seek a peaceful life and may be lazy at times unless given a good shove by other people. He is not a notable individualist; he enjoys being with others and will certainly like working with others. He seems particularly suited to PR work, diplomacy or the legal profession, though his mind may not be incisive enough for strenuously analytical tasks. He will have quite a lot to do with higher education in the course of his life, perhaps holding the chancellorship of a university or sitting on a royal commission on technical manpower in the year 2000!

Like any Cancer boy, he is close to his mother, and I expect him to marry someone similar to her, though not a Piscean – probably a Leo girl. The Venus–Saturn opposition suggests that he will not marry young – indeed, he may remain a bachelor until well into his thirties. But he'll be very much the ladies' man, and will have a long succession of eligible girlfriends.

The next child, Lady Helen Windsor, is fascinatingly like her second cousin Lady Sarah Armstrong-Jones. They were born within four days of each other, so the pattern of the sky is similar in each horoscope. Both of them enjoy this wonderful Sun–Mercury–Jupiter conjunction that provides such a sense of fun and *joie de vivre*. And, just as Sarah has the motherly sign of Cancer rising, so has Helen the motherly planet the Moon exactly on her Ascendant. These two girls will grow up with much inner rapport for each other, and this empathy – almost telepathy – will stay with them all their lives. But there will obviously be differences. Lady Helen will grow up with a strong interest in medicine, and will want to become a doctor, nurse or veterinary surgeon. I think her love of animals will be very strong. Like Sarah, she is a natural conservative, and will be greatly drawn to life in the countryside. She is quite an emotional girl, enthusiastic one moment and moody the next. It would not surprise me if she were affected by the Moon itself, especially at the time of the Full Moon. She is not a particularly logical or hard-headed girl, and she'll swap and change her ideas according to her heart's desires.

Helen will be attracted to two types of men. One will be cracker-jack type – witty, inventive, a bit unreliable – with whom she can enjoy frivolous arguments. The other type, whom she will take more seriously as a potential marriage partner, is the clever, ambitious, mature man who will provide security and act in some way as a father-figure. Helen is someone who can enjoy father-figures without actually *needing* them.

If George is the amiable gentleman and Helen the motherly tomboy, then Lord Nicholas Windsor, at present the baby of the family, will grow up to be the toughest and most determined of them all. It is possible that he is a slow developer – not mentally backward in any way, of course, but taking his time in allowing his true character to blossom. He has a lot in common with the Queen herself, since they share the same three signs as Ascendant, Sun-sign and Moon-sign, though not quite in the same order. Nicholas has the steady, stolid Capricorn rising, giving him a cool, reserved outer temperament. But there's a vivid Sun–Mercury–Mars conjunction in the bright, bouncy sign of Leo, so he's bound to have plenty to say for himself. He is the man who wants to take charge of a situation, and will do so in a charming and most decisive fashion. A business life will suit him well, except it will not provide enough outdoor life to satisfy him. And so, since the range of possible royal jobs is a restricted one, I daresay he will enjoy Army life as much as his father.

He is more of an individualist than he appears, at least as far as his work is concerned. I say he will be an *inspired* man at times, lifting himself and any men under his command to supercharged heights. He is one of those psychological types who appear cautious and steady in average conditions, but become inflamed with a special kind of magic whenever a crisis occurs.

He is another royal figure who is undoubtedly going to wield quite a sexual interest wherever he goes! With the Sun, Mercury and Mars all in the Seventh House, he'll have a great deal of fiery charm among the girls – but in himself he's very much a man's man. He could become rather overbearing and opinionated at times, so he needs to develop a little humility!

The oldest 'eligible royal bachelor' is these children's uncle, Prince Michael of Kent, now in his mid-thirties. He was born on 4 July 1942, only a month or so before his father was killed on a wartime flying mission. He was brought up without benefit of a strong paternal influence, and as a Cancerian he was bound to be under his mother's thumb, anyway. Not that he has become a mother's darling, by any means; he's an energetic, courageous sportsman in a number of fields, including ski-ing, bob-sleigh driving, and a dashing soldier to boot. But why has he never married?

There is one vivid and important planetary configuration in his birth-chart that could supply the answer. It's a close Venus–Saturn conjunction with an extra planet, Uranus, hovering nearby. This suggests a strong ambivalence in his attitude towards marriage. In one way, Saturn is encouraging him to settle down and form a secure, lasting partnership. In another, Uranus encourages him to remain independent. It also 'encourages' him – though he may not be a willing party here – to get into liaisons that are more than likely to break up. He has had a string of girlfriends and several of these have been older than himself. Certainly the Venus–Saturn conjunction makes him attracted to the adult kind of woman; certainly, too, as a Cancerian without a father he may be 'in thrall' with the Mother archetype. It is bound to have brought some disappointment to his love life, and made him wonder, at times, whether he has ever *truly* loved any of his girlfriends – for the Saturnian influence builds a wall around the heart which makes it hard for sweet, simple love to enter or leave.

Never mind, Venus moved by direction to his Sun in 1976, so he should have found the love of his life in that year.

His sister, Princess Alexandra, is greatly loved herself – not only by husband and family, of course, but by millions of nice, sentimental people throughout the country. They revere the Queen, and are bitchy about Margaret, but they adore Alexandra because she is so approachable and unsnobbish, with her own kind of gawky grace. She's a sort of super 'Girl-Next-Door', almost – dare I say it? – a royal Cilla Black.

Astrologically she's a mixture of tenderness and discipline. With Pisces rising, she gives a charming, willowy impression at first sight; but with Saturn on the eastern horizon, Sun in the tough sign of Capricorn and Moon in another Earth sign, Taurus, she is a much more capable and stubborn lady than she may appear. The softness is only a front; she can be formidable, frosty and determined. Obviously she is very conscious of doing her duty and hates the idea of stepping out of line. But certainly there are conflicts, with the planet Saturn fighting to maintain a sense of correctness while Pisces encourages her to be careless in little things.

Her marriage to Angus Ogilvy is solid, private and deeply cherishing. He's a dry, witty man, certainly not flamboyant or seeking publicity; by nature a City gent with directorships in his pocket and a hundred and one schemes for making money. It's appropriate that he should be a triple Virgoan, with the Ascendant, Sun and Moon all in this Zodiac sign. Shades of the Prince Consort! But Angus Ogilvy is saved from too frosty a demeanour by a nice charming Mercury–Venus conjunction.

Even so, he's a very Earthy man, and to the extent that they're almost identical, Princess Alexandra makes an admirable choice of partner for him. Both of them are practical and realistic people. Probably she has more imagination than he has, though will tend to say 'no' to an idea quicker than he would. He can be a single-minded man. I should think that a deep disagreement between them would be a fascinating psychological battle to watch. There would be lots of discreet manoeuvring and half-humorous, half-serious offers of compromise that would gradually edge them closer to harmony! Both of them are considerate, conscientious people. In a quarrel, they would hate to see the other party hurt, and so they are adept at allowing themselves room to lose with honour.

Their two children have some attractive qualities, too. James Ogilvy (born 29 February 1964 at 12.20 p.m.) is a Watery boy, with Cancer rising and the Sun in Pisces. This makes him sensitive and vulnerable, and at times he'll find his father in particular lacking in emotional *flow*. James has three striking conjunctions in his chart. A Sun–Mars conjunction makes him a hot-headed fellow at times, especially as Uranus is directly opposite; it looks as if the British public will have another racing-driver with royal connections! He will take to underwater-diving, too, as well as water-ski-ing and sailing.

Then there's a sweet Venus–Jupiter conjunction. He'll be a most popular young man, especially with the girls, and very generous and warm-hearted, too. This conjunction does give a gambling temperament at times, and this is certainly possible in James's case. But it stands in his Tenth House to do with career, so I cannot help feeling that he will work in a pleasing, artistic field. This could be fashion, restaurants, interior design or painting itself. He could become an expert in the fine arts and deal in pictures and furniture. I am sure he will be a man of parts, trying his hand at a variety of enterprises. He is not nearly so reliable and solid as his parents, and he will probably give them a few nervous worries once he starts living it up!

Finally there's a Mercury–Saturn conjunction which can work in two ways. Either it can lead to a distaste for further education (as in the case of Princess Anne) or a very plodding, conscientious attitude to work. James will probably develop a very good eye for detail, and may be an admirable draughtsman or even musician. But I do not think he is the naturally studious type.

His younger sister, Marina (born 31 July 1966, 7 p.m.), is a bit like her kinsman Lord Nicholas Windsor, as both have Capricorn rising and the Sun in Leo. I do not see her as quite such a dominant personality, however. There is a powerful aura of music attached to her horoscope, and with Neptune on the Midheaven she could have a promising future as a dancer, singer or keyboard performer. Like her brother James, she has a terrific Venus–Jupiter conjunction, with the added bonus of Mars to warm things up. Both of them will make happy and fulfilling marriages, but it's important that they avoid dull, upright people as partners. They seem such active and enterprising types themselves that they need plenty of emotional elbow-room to enjoy themselves.

Part Three **Future**

Future of the Royals

The idea that the future can be predicted gets some people in a terrible state. They feel trapped, imprisoned in a space–time continuum over which they have no control. They hate the notion that they have no free will over their life. And worst of all, they believe that life loses its point if you know the future, just as a play becomes boring if you've already read the story.

Surprising as it may seem for an astrologer to admit, I am one of these people. I do not want to have my whole life-span mapped out before my eyes, because it is important for my own self-respect to feel that I am in control of my own destiny. So, if I can't take my own medicine, why do I try to ram it down the throats of everyone else?

Normally, of course, I only make predictions for people who ask for a forecast. But in certain cases, the future of people in the public eye becomes a matter of public concern, and it's considered reasonable and proper to treat their horoscopes as public property. But there are limits, especially when we look at the private lives of celebrities. Suppose, for instance, I thought that one of the young up-and-coming Royals would turn out to be homosexual. Would it be seemly or helpful to make this conjecture public? Or suppose I asserted that the Queen would definitely die on such-and-such a date? Can you imagine Her Majesty's feelings when she reads my prediction? No, there has to be some caution exercised in these matters. And, besides, it simply isn't possible to be all that accurate. Usually I can get fairly near the truth, but rarely am I spot-on.

There are two principal areas of interest as far as the Royal Family is concerned. The first is a sentimental one – a deep and abiding interest in the everyday happenings of a group of people who are 'special' in the hearts of many millions of people throughout the world. This is treating the Royals like the inhabitants of *Coronation Street, Crossroads* or any other television soap opera. It's fascinating fun to see who will marry whom, how many children there will be, how so-and-so will grow old and whatever will happen to young Prince Marmaduke. At another level, we watch the Royal Family in the same way that we follow motor-racing or some daring circus act. We are really waiting for disaster to strike – waiting for the *frisson* of horror when the car bursts into flames, the trapeze artist crashes to the ground, or the British Throne is swept away in the swirling throes of a political revolution. Will they all be shot to death in Buckingham Palace courtyard? Or will Charles the Last follow Charles the First to the scaffold? Or will they end their days in decent exile in Australia, surfing and drinking lager and singing *Tie Me Kangaroo Down* along with the rest of the population?

Several broad long-term predictions can be made about the Royal Family. They will find it increasingly hard to maintain public interest in what may be called the Windsor Saga because: (i) there has been a sharp and irreversible shift towards much greater social equality in Britain, and (ii) the younger members of the Family will have nothing specifically to contribute to national life in the 1980s and 1990s. Once the public sees too many privileged people being kept by the State, they will get resentful.

This probable shift towards republicanism in Britain will certainly be mirrored by a loss of royal influence throughout the Commonwealth. Her Majesty is constitutionally as much Queen of Australia as Queen of Canada, but she has steadfastly refused to live for any length of time in either country – nor any other of her territories besides the United Kingdom. With Britain itself rapidly becoming a third-rate industrial force in the world, and the focus of international events shifting away from the old imperial white nations towards the yellow ones bordering the Pacific, the usefulness of the Crown will disappear. If the countries of the Commonwealth increasingly feel the need to assert their own national identities, and the United Kingdom itself disappears within a Federal States of Europe, what place can there be for the ancient British Throne?

The logic of events is obviously towards the extinction of our token monarchy. Once the currency loses its value, nobody uses it any more. So it's up to the monarchy itself to work out how -- and why -- it can survive. Can it retain, or enhance, its 'entertainment value' as attractive, well-mannered people to whom the public naturally responds with warmth and pleasure? And can it maintain its 'mythic value' as embodiments of the *real Britain*, almost as figureheads of the British archetype?

It can only keep its show-business appeal if the individual family members become personalities in their own right. They needn't, indeed shouldn't, be cast in the same mould, which is a criticism that can be made of the present adult Royals. A script editor for the *Windsor Saga* would devise a nice contrast of characters for the next royal series. He would pick a bright, vivacious, slightly unconventional wife for Charles (quite possibly American, to sell the show in the States); at least one baddie among the current crop of young Royals; perhaps one excessively virtuous goodie (a royal monk -- now *there*'s a touch of genius); and certainly three or four major surprises surrounding the Royal Family in the next twenty years. There could be the threat of an unsuitable marriage; a controversy involving politics; perhaps a shady business deal; and even that great standard of popular fiction, an attempted kidnap or assassination.

So much for entertainment. If the Royal Family is to keep its mythic appeal, there will need to be two developments affecting the British people. The first is a war -- not a short, cataclysmic nuclear holocaust, of course, but a drawn-out siege where the threatened country can draw strength and moral purpose from the example of the monarch. The other is a kind of spiritual renewal within Britain that sees Her Majesty and her children as genuinely powerful figures radiating goodness and light.

What has astrology to say about these possible developments in the future? With Uranus and later Pluto in the deep, explosive sign of Scorpio, the world in the rest of the 1970s and 1980s will be a dangerous place. If I were asked to name a planetary configuration that signified a nuclear war, this would be it. But equally, I expect a deep, shattering spiritual awakening to burst out from the Pluto-in-Scorpio position in the 1980s and 1990s. The ancient spiritual fire that burns in certain parts of the world --

Britain included – will be rekindled, and people will look to the British Isles for some kind of inspiration. But whether the Royal Family is part of this development it is much harder to say.

At a more personal level, I believe the Royal Family will provide a lot of interest – and at times controversy – in the next ten or twenty years. I base this assertion on a close study of all their horoscopes, using not only directions and transits but also more sophisticated techniques such as secondary progressions and midpoint analysis.

The remainder of this book is devoted to a year-by-year forecast of the Royal Family's fortunes for the next fifteen years. Two points should be made about these predictions. My statements are a kind of guesswork based on detailed astrological fact. Whenever I say 'will happen', I mean 'could reasonably correspond with the astrological influences in force at the time'. And of course the unexpected can occur to throw out all my calculations. Any member of the Royal Family could die tomorrow, making my predictions for him (or her) for the next few years look pretty silly! And of course I can't predict the future of any as-yet-unborn royal children. I need to know their birthdays for that!

The Final Years

1977

This looks like a year of royal celebrations. Not only will the
Queen have her Silver Jubilee – having sat on the Throne for
twenty-five years – but two young men will probably get married:
Prince Charles and Prince Michael of Kent.

Although Charles has stated that he does not intend to marry
before the age of thirty, I believe he has already met and fallen in
love with the future Queen of England. Their romance will
have leaked unofficially in the summer of 1976, but the wedding
itself will take place in the autumn of 1977.

His bride will be English upper–middle-class, probably an old
friend of the family.

Prince Michael will plan marriage, too. His wife may not be
English, and could be the daughter of a wealthy European
businessman. His wedding will be a relatively quiet affair, and he
may decide to leave the Army and spend more time abroad.

There's bad news for the Royal Family, too. Saturn plays a big
part in their horoscopes in 1977, particularly in the case of the
Queen and Queen Elizabeth the Queen Mother. This could be a
tricky year for the Queen Mum, and she may well have to take
life much more carefully in the years to come. February to May
1977 is a particularly trying time when she feels cooped up and
frustrated, and during the same period the Queen will feel very
responsible and protective towards her mother.

Another possibility is that the Queen herself could be ill,
perhaps with a complaint that is not made public. The Jubilee
celebrations may be a special trial to her. Security arrangements
will be specially tight, and this will prove irksome to Elizabeth
who likes, certainly, to feel safe but not constrained.

Princess Anne may give birth to a baby in late summer or autumn

1977. A key date seems to be August or early September. This would make the child a Virgoan like its father, with Venus very close to its own position in Princess Anne's horoscope. This indicates a warm, loving relationship between parents and child, though a big bouncy Leo girl such as Anne may find two Virgoans in the family rather trying in years to come; they do worry so much.

The same month, August, sees an end to the difficult Pluto transit that has been plaguing Princess Margaret for the last year or two. It began in 1976 and has stayed in force ever since. This exact transit to Venus has marked a divorce-type situation in her marriage. If an actual divorce is to follow her legal separation from Lord Snowdon, then the decision could well be taken now.

Of course another relationship could be involved – a friendship that has run its course and now come to a tricky make-or-break phase. Princess Margaret may be faced by yet another agonizing choice between pleasure and duty.

1978

The start of 1978 is a problematic time for two lesser Royals, Angus Ogilvy and his brother-in-law the Duke of Kent. Early in 1976 the Duke decided to leave the Army to take up a post boosting British exports. One reason may have been that he felt frustrated in the modern Army, but a more likely explanation is that he needed to earn more money than his Army salary.

I believe that the Duke will be changing his job yet again, thanks to Pluto conjunct his Sun and Saturn conjunct his Ascendant. It is certainly an anxious, responsible time for both men – an apt moment for them to go into business together. But Mr Ogilvy should be warned that a clever business scheme could backfire on him at this time. Black Africa, the Far East, the West Indies – anywhere that political trouble could have an adverse effect on his business interests – are the areas that he should seek to avoid.

February looks a particularly jolly time for Princess Anne – an excellent month for a winter holiday (or royal tour) away from Britain. The United States and Caribbean islands would be a sensible region to visit.

Later in the year she will be busy with preparations to open her own business in horses: training, breeding, providing facilities to encourage younger riders. She could help to promote a business venture tied to one of the stately homes of England.

The Queen has a restful time in the spring, when she may take one of her comparatively rare private visits out of Britain. She will become patron of a new charity connected with the preservation of the British way of life. But there is some trouble attached to an organization with which she has links. One obvious possibility is the Royal Society for the Prevention of Cruelty to Animals, which may vote to dissociate itself from royalty due to fox-hunting and other blood sports. Another possibility is that one of the Silver Jubilee trusts will run into financial difficulty, and the Queen's name will be slightly tarnished, even though she is not personally to blame.

The Duke of Edinburgh has a tricky time in April, when Saturn forms a station close to his Moon. Part of the anxiety will stem from royal finances. There will be detailed discussions with the Government about whether the Royal Household should become a department of State, and the Duke – to say nothing of the Queen herself! – will worry about the Privy Purse moving out of the Queen's control.

This will be an interesting year for the Duke of Gloucester. A Sun–Midheaven aspect suggests that he will feel happier in his work. He will form a new partnership, perhaps with several other young architects, with the task of providing modern extensions to ancient buildings. He may be involved in a lecture tour of the United States.

Charles will be thirty years old in the autumn. This looks a wonderfully exciting time for him. His Jupiter–Uranus opposition will be triggered into action, and he may undertake a daring but successful experiment involving air travel. Jupiter enters his First House in October, so for the next year he will enjoy a big measure of personal popularity and fulfilment. He will be deeply in love at this time – especially in late October when he will be bursting with affection and love. This could mark the birth of a child (provided he married in 1977!) – otherwise it's the right moment for a wedding if there was any kind of delay the year before.

1979

This could be a crucial year for the Queen Mother, with Pluto forming a conjunction with her Ascendant. Her life shifts into a new gear. There could be domestic rearrangements in her life in April and possible recuperative travel in June, but by December she reaches a point of no return. This could be an illness which radically changes her lifestyle.

By this time, Prince Andrew will be at university – probably Cambridge, like his brother, reading Modern History. He will be very active in amateur dramatics and possibly one of the martial arts: karate or fencing. He may also make one or two indiscreet speeches at the Union. After the rigours of Gordonstoun, he will enjoy the freedom of university. His egotism will be more apparent.

Lord Snowdon – or Tony Armstrong-Jones as he wishes to be called now – makes some important changes in his career. For part of the year he will be engrossed in making a film that takes him right away from civilization for many months – up in the polar north, for instance – and this could involve him in political problems, especially if his work takes him to Finland and Siberia. This could faintly embarrass the Royal Family, even though Tony will no longer consider himself part of the royal set. He could give an outspoken interview concerning royal residences and the homeless. His influence not only on his own children but his nephews Prince Andrew and Prince Edward will be fairly strong: a slight case of hero worship by the young Royals. His own boy David will feel specially close to Tony, and will accompany him on one of his overseas forays, somewhat to the alarm of Princess Margaret.

The Queen has a particularly pleasant July. This may be relief at her mother's partial recovery in these summer months, but there will also be special pride on behalf of her children. She could become a grandmother again in August, when Princess Anne has a Moon–Saturn conjunction and a Jupiter–Sun conjunction. This nicely corresponds with a difficult confinement and a happy outcome. Any child born in the third week, around the 17th, is likely to be a girl with strong links with Anne herself, of course, since her birthday is two days earlier, on the 15th.

Princess Alexandra will be in the news in the autumn, possibly due to a narrow escape from an accident. It may be that her name will be involved in some other newsworthy matter. Perhaps she will be mentioned in a court case as the friend of the accused, or in some society scandal it will be revealed that Alexandra is slightly – and innocently – involved.

Prince Philip becomes involved in a cause that would not normally be associated with royalty. It could bring him into confrontation with British trades union bosses, and some sharp words will be exchanged in newspapers.

1980

Anne and Mark's business as trainers and breeders will be doing well. His mother, Mrs Peter Phillips, will play an important role in this work. Anne herself will not be jumping competitively this year, due to a small but annoying injury during practice in March. Mark will go abroad on his own for a month or two in the early summer, probably to visit the United States, and this will result in American financial backing which is unlikely to be made public at the time.

And yet the Royal Family must always be careful about their finances, especially when it seems that a profit could be made out of using the royal name. It may be that the Phillips's will form a consortium with several other upper-crust show-jumpers so that their own involvement isn't so blatant that it appears they are trading on their royal connections.

There will probably be a royal robbery in 1980. One of the Queen's palaces will be broken into, possibly in October, and some considerable damage could be caused and royal possessions dating back to Georgian times be stolen.

The alternative is that the strict net of security surrounding Her Majesty is broken. SPY AT BUCKINGHAM PALACE makes an arresting headline, but it is unlikely to be as simple as that. But it could be that lines of communication between the Queen and her principal ministers at Downing Street and the Foreign Office are 'interfered with'. Or one of the famous red boxes in which Elizabeth receives her State papers daily will go astray.

Viscount Lindley will leave school. It is unlikely that he will go straight to university, if at all, and will probably work abroad for a year under the artistic direction of one of his father's friends. I feel France or Italy is his most likely country of residence. David will enjoy a vivid late adolescent period when the glories of the past, particularly Renaissance art, will come truly alive for him. He will be keen to put ideas down on paper, in words and drawings, but his problem will be this: he will find things too easy, and want to make them 'serious' and 'difficult'. So he may invent problems where none exists.

Princess Alexandra will have trouble with her back. With Saturn rising, she is always liable to problems connected with bones, and regular visits to an osteopath will from now on be necessary. She and her husband will become good friends with an up-and-coming politician. Although this link may not become public for many years, it will be an important friendship; and when he finally attains high office, they will feel, rightly or wrongly, that their *protégé* has come good.

The Queen will propose a special celebratory gathering of European Heads of State in connection with the European Economic Community. The EEC will be poised in a delicate state. To some observers it will be on the brink of shattering into fragments; to others it will be tottering towards greater political union, and the Queen's move will be designed to promote unity and greater harmony among member states.

There are strong links between Her Majesty's horoscope and South Africa, so it is possible there will be a much warmer atmosphere between Britain and the Republic by 1980. One explanation for this is that the Republic is no more, having been superceded by a black majority government, but I think this unlikely. More probable is the idea that the South African Government has become increasingly inter-racial; and in addition, the threat of the Russian Navy to the sea-route round the Cape has necessitated greater friendship between the Western allies and South Africa.

Princess Margaret should be happier. She will not greatly enjoy the late 1970s, due to the presence of Saturn in her birth-sign, but by now she should be launched into a new venture with some enthusiasm. Possibly a schoolgirl hobby of her daughter, Lady Sarah, will have grabbed her attention. This will involve country life, away from the bustle of London.

1981

The Duke of Gloucester will be involved in a controversy this year. He will be speaking quite passionately on a cause close to his heart, and this could upset the Establishment in some way.

March will produce a change in royal living arrangements. I believe that one of the royal palaces will be given to the nation, and will be open to the public during the 1980s. This will be part of the necessary royal economies following the 'nationalization' of the Queen's cash situation.

At the same time, Her Majesty will spend some months abroad, probably in Canada.

Prince Andrew will be a very lively young man at Cambridge. By this time he will be rebelling against his royal background and developing some out-of-the-ordinary ideas of his own. His romantic life will hit the headlines in May and June when Uranus makes an interesting contact with his Mars–Venus conjunction. This could involve a scandal of some sort. He will be eager for exciting experiences at this time, or a promising friendship will be dashed through impulsive behaviour. There is no doubt that Andrew, like his Auntie Margaret, has an appetite for the bizarre, due to the important planet Uranus in their birth-charts. But with this planet making a contact to the aggressive planet Mars as well as the loving Venus, Andrew is likely to get angry, worked up, even a little violent. He could get quite a shock.

Lady Sarah Armstrong-Jones will probably leave Bedales for art school. She will want to be involved with nursing, but her parents will suggest that she does not make it her full-time career.

The Prince of Wales will be happily married by this time, certainly with one child and possibly two – but this depends on the horoscope of his wife, which we do not yet know. He will no longer be a full-time naval officer. He will appear on television in his role of comedian, publish a book which he has written in collaboration with an expert and take a personal interest in a national problem to do with pollution of some sort: car exhausts, smoking, reservoirs or perhaps noise.

He may also find that he is being used as a political pawn in the Welsh devolution argument, which will become much stronger in the 1980s as soon as Celtic Sea oil is discovered in marketable quantities.

His brother Edward faces a difficult autumn. In November the planet Saturn crosses his Ascendant. Probably he will not be working hard enough at school and will be given a stern pep-talk. But he will also receive extra responsibility, which will make him inwardly anxious and worried. He may also be the victim of a nasty infectious disease: a new virus mutation that will sweep through Britain in the winter of 1981–2.

1982

Throughout most of this year, Prince Andrew continues in a rebellious mood, with Uranus square to his Sun and Pluto threatening his Midheaven. If he joins the Royal Air Force, which he is likely to do as a result of family pressure – after all, every royal male must have his quota of service duty – he will feel trapped by the training and discipline required. His rebellion could take several forms. First, he may well have pronounced political views – along radical lines, of course – which he will not be discreet enough to keep to himself. Secondly, he will want to follow a particular lifestyle that does not accord with conventional upper-crust behaviour. This could affect his diet, dress and even his religious life, for Pluto on the Midheaven frequently involves some kind of spiritual conversion. Andrew, for instance, could become deeply committed to a new cult developing in Britain in the 1980s, but I doubt whether he will gladly accept religious discipline any more than military orders.

There are signs of some disagreement with his mother the Queen in the summer of 1982, and he may uproot himself from the family in some way.

Philip's chart is likely to be affected by Neptune during the early 1980s, especially this year. He will become slightly adrift in his direction in life. He will play less part in public life, and more time away by himself. He will certainly become much more sensitive and perhaps irritable when disturbed. Music will start to mean a great deal to him — more than it has ever done in his life — and religion will have an added significance. Whether this brings him into conflict with — or closer to — his son Andrew remains to be seen. My guess is that he will feel out of touch with Andrew so he must let the lad go his own way.

The Queen has an otherwise good year. There could well be a new Prime Minister this year in Britain. Mrs Margaret Thatcher is certainly involved in the changes, though whether she's in or out of Downing Street is a moot point. My guess is that there will be a new leader of the Tory Party in 1982, someone who will quickly establish a warm and friendly relationship with his monarch. There will be a shift of policy that will heartily meet with the Queen's approval.

Princess Anne will be riding with great success in July and August, which bodes well for her inclusion in the European Championships. A more troubling time will be October, when Saturn reaches her Ascendant. One of her children could have an acute infection which makes her depressed and worried.

The same influence will bring problems to Viscount Lindley. Venus will have reached his Sun just as he leaves his teens and enters his twenties, so he will be deeply in love — especially in November 1982 when Jupiter conjoins Mars. So he will want to marry young, but be deeply unsure whether he should make such a choice. He has the experience of his parents to remember, and children of a broken home are usually unwilling to commit themselves quickly to marriage. Perhaps he will simply live with the girl, and once the Press get to know about this, there will be plenty of hypocritical shock in the editorial columns to boost the circulation.

1983

The Queen gets embroiled in a dual constitutional crisis. Internal devolution will have brought Scotland to the point of no return in her dealings with Westminster. The Scottish Assembly, meeting in Edinburgh, may pass a motion questioning whether the monarchy is serving any useful role in their nation.

European integration, on the other hand, will bring to the forefront of public attention the idea of a Head of State for Europe as a whole. Possibly the EEC President will be acting in too political a manner, and people will declare in favour of a strictly constitutional Head of State for the emerging European Federation.

Whether their two problems actually develop into a 'crisis' in 1983 remains to be seen. Nothing may be settled for years to come, but the Queen will feel marginally less secure on the Throne. Soon, she will sense, she may not rule over Scotland. Soon, indeed, constitutional control may move from Buckingham Palace to Brussels, Strasbourg or some other European capital.

The Prince and Princess of Wales will make a world tour. Charles's chart shows extensive journeyings during 1983, with special emphasis on the Far East, including China. The main purpose will, naturally, be to show the flag. China and Britain will have reached agreement over the long-term future of Hong Kong, and Charles will be anxious to cement this new-found friendship with the Chinese. On a personal note, he will be fascinated by certain aspects of Chinese life, especially in the field of industrial cooperation between management and workers, and he will come back full of enthusiasm for adapting some of these methods to the British way of life.

August brings a fine moment of success to Prince Andrew – probably in a dangerous sport he has taken up. He will also win family agreement on the next stage of his career.

There is a very happy influence affecting both Princess Margaret and her former husband Tony Armstrong-Jones. It is very unlikely that it will mean that they will become reconciled, but they could share some happiness together – say as a result of the birth of a grandchild if their son David has married, or some moment of success enjoyed by their daughter Lady Sarah. Equally likely, both Tony and Margaret in their separate ways should be happy in their emotional lives. If, as is likely, a divorce has already taken place in the late 1970s, Tony could well remarry in 1983. Margaret, too, could have formed a deep, private relationship. She is unlikely to marry again, but she could well spend a certain amount of time – unknown to the general public – with her new friend.

1984

Prince Andrew's progress will continue to be erratic. An activity which he began in high hopes in 1983 will fizzle out a few months later. His social behaviour will still puzzle a number of people. Undoubtedly he has talent, they will say, but he throws it into such odd enterprises. Andrew will have access to his own funds by this stage, and could well be associated with making films. He could make a stunning profit through some kind of cinematic partnership. He will also put money into other ventures, including possibly a restaurant or even a theatre. If his Piscean nature draws him strongly to the sea, his name could also be associated with a marina.

By September Prince Andrew will have discovered an absorbing creative activity that fills him with elation. Pluto forms a trine to his Sun, signifying that he will find his true destiny this year.

The Prince of Wales will move house. In the face of rising criticism from the Commonwealth, he may decide to spend an extensive period in Australia, taking over the role of Governor-General. Although the Australians will be predominantly republican at heart by this stage, they will take the Prince and his young family to their heart. Another member of the Royal Family making himself at home in Australia will be Uncle Tony; he could well be in charge of a large cultural complex in Sydney or Melbourne. Lord Lindley will join him out there for a while.

The Royal Family, as a whole, faces a difficult time at the end of 1984. The planet Saturn forms a conjunction with Charles's Sun and his mother's Midheaven in the closing months of the year, while Pluto will have been opposite Her Majesty's Sun in the September before.

One possibility is ill-health. The Queen will be fifty-eight years old, and could have an operation that would involve Charles taking over the reins of Acting Regent for a while. Inevitably this could rebound on his Australian visit. The Aussies would not take kindly to their own Governor-General being whisked back to London only a few months after his arrival.

Another possibility is that the hereditary line of accession will be questioned by Parliament. There will be calls for a referendum to establish whether the monarchy could be elected, like a presidency. This is strongly bound up with Scottish independence. If the United Kingdom starts to disintegrate, with Ulster returning to Eire and Scotland claiming its own nationhood, the role of the Crown will be seriously weakened. The crisis begins in September and continues until Christmas, but it will be satisfactorily resolved, by a curious coincidence, on New Year's Day 1985.

I believe this will be the date of a new constitution for the United Kingdom.

1985

This is an important year for the Queen. Jupiter passing through her First House suggests that she will receive a lot of admiration, and that she will be travelling more than usual. But Saturn on her Midheaven throughout the year indicates that she is bearing a heavy responsibility at this time. I believe she will be carrying out special duties as appointed head of the European Federation. Each Head of State of the member-states will take it in turn to hold this honour, and the Queen, as the longest reigning Head of State in the continent, will be invited to be first.

In addition, there will be continued difficulties within the United Kingdom itself. It is possible that with devolution gathering pace, the Queen will be under pressure to relinquish her personal reign over Scotland and Wales. Her second son, Andrew, provided he has settled down to a serious contemplation of affairs of state, might be asked to act as Head of State of Scotland. The Queen herself would not welcome this move, feeling that the young man is too inexperienced to act as her representative in the independent nation of Scotland; but some of her ministers may feel that it is the best solution in a final effort to keep the Scots somehow within the United Kingdom.

Prince Charles will certainly be against Andrew – probably now called the Duke of Cambridge – taking on State duties while he as heir to the Throne waits patiently in the wings to take on the role of monarch at the appropriate time. There could be numerous differences between the two brothers this year. Charles is much the steadier of the two; he can go deeper into issues and has a wider vision in State matters. Andrew is a much more superficially imaginative man, more influenced than Charles by glamour and self-importance. Charles in the end will win the argument, but Andrew is not someone who can readily accept defeat.

Prince Edward, by now twenty-one years old, will enjoy a wonderful year. He will be having a splendid time in the Royal Navy, and Uranus contacting his Mercury suggests that he will be involved in a special new form of transportation: perhaps a nuclear warship, or a giant naval hovercraft.

Lord Snowdon will start an important new job this year, probably connected with a television service. This could be in his favourite warm climate, Australia, or linked with the United States. His eyesight will be causing problems, and he may undergo a small operation. His son David will be associated with him in his work. His daughter Sarah will be travelling, spending some months on the continent, especially France, where she will get into a swinging set that will hit the headlines. But she is such a sensible young lady that she is unlikely to go off the rails.

Princess Margaret will be connected with the art world in some way. She may sponsor a small exhibition of someone whose talent she wishes to promote. She may think of moving out of Kensington Palace altogether. If certain members of Parliament continue to criticize her behaviour (such as lack of public duties) she may arrange to defend herself for the first time on television. A young friend of hers may make a documentary film about Her Royal Highness. It will be a complimentary portrait – but then he may spoil the image by trying to make too much money out of the film.

1986

Prince Philip is the member of the Royal Family most in the news this year. Uranus opposite his Sun, and Pluto hovering near his Midheaven, indicate some crucial changes in his life. Although he will be a mere sixty-five years old, it is possible that an illness could strike. With Uranus active, symptoms could develop quickly. Mid—March is the time he is most prone to a sudden attack. Alternatively, an operation may be necessary at this time.

Leaving ill-health aside, it is certain that some kind of upheaval will come the Prince's way. Uranus means that he will be edgy, restless and keen to break away from everyday responsibilities. Pluto on his Midheaven means a significant change in his career. So he may simply 'retire', still playing some role in public life but increasingly private. This doesn't sound like the Duke of Edinburgh at all – so illness remains a real possibility.

Since Pluto will also be square to the position of Venus in the Queen's horoscope, it will be a time of some strain for the Queen. A probable explanation of these planetary configurations is Philip's 'retirement' of some sort.

The summer of 1986 will be an important time for Princess Anne. With Saturn making a trine to her Sun, it will be a time of responsibility and success through hard effort. By this stage she could be manager of a group of show-jumpers, perhaps in charge of the British show-jumping team itself, and if so she will be leading them to victory.

Mark's chart is also involved in a similar way, so the pair of them are likely to be deeply engrossed in some difficult project. This could be a successful business venture. It could, just possibly, be a happy outcome to a difficult pregnancy. Anne will be thirty-six by this stage, and at that age all sorts of complications can arise.

March and April will be good months for Prince Andrew. At the age of twenty-six he will have matured a good deal. He will have been a success in at least one traditional sphere of royal duty, and his personality and charm will have been greatly appreciated by gossip columnists, young ladies of fashion, and the public at large. The British public will no longer be alarmed by Andrew; they will know that underneath his mischievous and sometimes arrogant exterior there is a basic commonsense and decency. Nonetheless, he will still be something of an *enfant terrible*. In the spring of 1986 he will cause something of a sensation by springing a surprise on everyone. It may involve a romance, but he will not actually marry this year. That will be reserved for the early 1990s.

Lady Helen Windsor, daughter of the Duke of Kent, will also be in the news. Newspapers will try to link her name romantically with young Prince Andrew, but in fact they do not have much in common. She may well spend time with some glamorous American film star, and pay a visit to Hollywood as a result, but nothing serious will come of it.

1987

The Duke of Kent enjoys a particularly lucky year. Something wonderful out of the blue could come his way. It will make him feel prosperous and successful at the same time.

It could be that an invitation will suddenly arrive, something unexpected and rather flattering. It may produce a conflict between his business activities and his royal duty, and it will be necessary for him to put his financial affairs in the hands of an impartial adviser for a while. The British Government may have a special task for him to undertake, such as chairing a Royal Commission or taking charge of a delicate constitutional role. The Government, due to the personal outlook of the Prime Minister of the day, will be very keen to involve members of the Royal Family in more than simply ceremonial roles in public life.

His son, the Earl of St Andrews, will be in his mid-twenties. A controversy surrounds him in 1987. Possibly he will take part in an expedition that gets momentarily lost in the wilds of Outer Ruritania. He seems to emerge as a hero, with a great deal of popularity around him. The alternative is a great sporting success.

Prince Edward should be falling in love and getting lots of gossip columnists on his tail. It is possible that he will be a little indiscreet, going through a great courtship ritual . . . and then failing to pop the question to the poor girl. This could continue for a year or so, until the affair fizzles out. I have a feeling that the girl involved could be foreign, perhaps French, with connections in high places, like being the daughter of a French politician or business tycoon.

Queen Elizabeth will have been thirty-five years on the Throne, and this year she will have reached sixty-one years of age. Inevitably there will have been a great deal of discussion about her abdication in favour of Prince Charles, but nothing definite will have emerged.

It will become known that the Queen is engaged in writing her memoirs, not necessarily as a book but as a series of interviews that will not be shown until long after her death. But she may feel, once her ideas are committed to film, that they are simply too gossipy, and that she has nothing particularly remarkable or noteworthy to tell future generations. So her own sense of conservatism will encourage her to destroy what has already been recorded. Hopefully, wiser counsels will prevail . . .

Princess Margaret has an interesting, yet indefinable year. With Neptune passing over her Midheaven in 1985–6, she will increasingly wish to withdraw from public life. In addition, her religious attitudes, which are sometimes so influential in shaping her activities, will once again play an important role in her thinking.

Psychologically she will be striving to discover a new meaning to life. With Neptune evident, this should make her a more humble person, subduing the Leo desire to be queen of all she surveys!

Tony Armstrong-Jones, meanwhile, has Uranus hovering around his Midheaven all year. He is bound to be deeply involved in making movies at this time. However diffident he appears on the surface, Tony is a strong-willed individual who can have a surprising effect on people he works with. I expect him to play a crucial role in shaping the ideas of young people in the late 1980s.

1988

Princess Alexandra has the doubtful pleasure of Saturn on her Sun in April of this year, and by December it's joined by Uranus.

This suggests that the normally well-balanced and placid Princess will be fussing and fretting when she reaches her fifties. In some extraordinary way, she will seek to change her lifestyle. Since her husband Angus reaches his sixtieth birthday this year, they will probably decide to retire, spending much more time away from public life. Their children, James and Marina, will both be grown up, well able to look after themselves, so they will have no pressing reasons for remaining in London – or even Britain.

I get a hunch that the country of their choice could be Switzerland or Austria.

This is an important year for the Duke of Gloucester. With Pluto on his ruler Mercury and the Midheaven by direction on Venus, he will be involved in some very exhausting but satisfying artistic project. He will have a difficult job forcing his ideas on other people. One likely event will be that the Duke will be involved in a propaganda campaign. He could become a principal spokesman for a new agricultural technique that he has employed on his Northants estate; but more probably he will be urging the preservation of a particular set of buildings.

It is an admirable time for him to write and publish a major book on architecture.

Mid-1988 is a tricky time for the Prince of Wales. High hopes will be dashed, and he will suffer a disappointment. This could be a personal matter, but more probably it will be linked to a political objective about which he had been optimistic. It is possible that pressure will be put on Parliament to include the Prince's own possessions, including the valuable Duchy of Cornwall lands, within the ambit of legislation before the Commons. Until now, the monarch and her immediate family have been exempt from legislation, on the grounds that the Crown cannot pass laws against itself. But the new spirit of republicanism will sweep this old concept aside. The upshot may be that the Prince of Wales will lose effective control over his lands, especially if all farming land and forestry estates are gradually brought under nationalized control in the late 1980s.

A highly left-wing government would be naturally antagonistic towards royalty in general and perhaps the Queen in particular, for by this stage in her reign she will have become associated with all aspects of life that are considered 'anti-progressive'.

Despite these pressures, Elizabeth will enjoy a good 1988. Once again, the planet Jupiter will pass through her First House, as it did in the first year of her reign back in 1952. And just as her presence and personality seemed, in those far-off days, to usher in a new Elizabethan Age, so it is possible that she will once more exert some magnetism of character over the British people to make her a popular, well-loved figure, even if her government is against her.

Remember that 1988 will be the four-hundredth anniversary of the Spanish Armada. It would be an appropriate gesture if Queen Elizabeth II journeyed to Tilbury to give a jingoistic, rousing speech, just as her ancestor Elizabeth I did on the eve of the Spanish invasion.

1989

An oddly uneventful year for the Royals. The only notable occasion will be the wedding of either Lady Sarah Armstrong-Jones or Lady Helen Windsor.

The republican mood will continue in certain quarters. The latest victim would seem to be Princess Margaret. With Uranus on her Midheaven, she will be a spitfire in reply. By this time, the traditional royal reticence in the face of attack will have lessened, and Margaret will be quite ready and able to reply to her critics. At a positive level, she will have something of real merit and importance to give to the British people this year. I feel that she will be appearing quite often on television, once she has discovered the knack of being relaxed and natural.

Another person whose chart is vibrating with inner astrological significance is Prince Charles. The planet Uranus will have travelled half-way round the sky since his moment of birth, so that it will be exactly opposite his position at birth. The last time this configuration was brought into effect was the moment of his investiture as Prince of Wales. At that time, it was greatly feared that Charles would be assassinated by Welsh Nationalists. As it turned out, he must have received a great measure of spiritual illumination as a result of this ancient ceremony.

So again in 1989, Charles could have a narrow escape from disaster. Three planets – Uranus, Saturn and Jupiter – are involved, and the meaning of this planetary grouping is the urge to break out of a rut – or the need to calm down. At best, Charles could become the catalyst enabling a British invention to receive the funds to be further researched and developed.

1990

Prince Andrew is in luck. Jupiter forms a long, deeply satisfying station on his Ascendant during the latter half of 1990. At the same time, there's a super sexy Mars–Venus contact by direction and, even better, a Jupiter–Venus conjunction. So he must be blissfully in love.

But a gamble's involved. The dark planet Saturn sits on the Queen's Ascendant in November 1990, just when Andrew should be at his happiest. Of course, the two astrological events need not be connected. The Queen could simply be feeling sad and worried about something else – a personal illness, perhaps, or a political problem connected with Parliament. But equally she could be feeling anxious about Andrew's choice of bride. As mother and head of the family, she will be very cautious and 'traditional' at this time, so Andrew should not attempt too radical a choice. But he will be past the age of consent (twenty-five) required by law, so Andrew can marry whom he pleases, with or without the Queen's blessing.

Mark Phillips may also be having his share of problems. Starting in 1989, Mark has a Venus–Pluto square corresponding to a tense emotional situation. This certainly does not necessarily mean that Anne and Mark will be unhappy: it may simply be a tricky time for both of them. Both will be in their early forties, and this can be a tiresome time for many couples after many years of marriage.

Jupiter, the planet ruling love affairs in his horoscope, lies in the Twelfth House of secrecy during 1989–90. In March and April of this year, an awkward Mercury–Saturn square suggests that he will be under a good deal of mental pressure; and at the same time the dark planet Saturn is hovering opposite Anne's Venus, indicating some unhappiness in her life.

But it looks as though the whole matter can be happily resolved in time. By the end of the year, Jupiter will have moved into Mark's First House, indicating much joy and sense of freedom in his life; and by the following year, Jupiter reaches Anne's Sun, too.

1991

Saturn continues in the Queen's First House, causing quite deep depression and sense of responsibility. If Philip has already died – or needs much care and cherishing – Elizabeth will find the duties of her office very heavy to bear. It is equally possible that the whole Royal Family is under a cloud.

In contrast to this, Charles's popularity should be strong and growing. Thanks to the presence of Jupiter on his Ascendant in the spring of 1991, he should feel confident and self-assured about his place in life. Possibly the Queen will have imparted privately to him the information that she will abdicate the following year. Possibly, too, he personally will be in favour with the British Parliament, even though the Royal Family as a whole are considered rather wasteful parasites.

I expect there will be strong pressure for the Queen to abdicate. She will soon have reigned for forty years, and will be surrounded by ministers and fellow Heads of State who were still at kindergarten whilst she was studying State papers at Buckingham Palace.

There is a further problem in Anne and Mark's horoscopes. In April the planet Saturn will be on the cusp of Mark's Seventh House, to do with marriage and other close relationships. Saturn will also be affecting Anne's Midheaven.

1992

This is the crucial year for the Prince of Wales and, by implication, the whole Royal Family. He will undergo a deep and important change, due to Pluto moving from a square aspect at birth to an exact conjunction with his Sun. This was the transit that accompanied Princess Margaret's declaration that she would not marry Group Captain Peter Townsend. Some similar kind of sacrifice may be required from Charles. That, or a calling to some ineluctable destiny.

Bear in mind that Pluto contacts not only Charles's Sun in 1992–3 but also the Queen's Midheaven, Prince Philip's Moon, Princess Anne's Sun, Prince Andrew's Moon and Prince Edward's Midheaven, as well as planets in the horoscopes of lesser members of the Royal Family.

There are four possibilities to account for the conglomeration of influences at this time:

1. The Queen will die, leaving the Throne to Charles. This is obviously a possibility, but in a way the influences are too heavy and lugubrious simply to correspond with a quiet little demise. There is a strong air of crisis and crucial decisions involved.

2. Charles will die, leaving Andrew as heir. This is only possible if he died in some extraordinary, 'meant' way. To be honest, Pluto does not necessarily correspond with ordinary dying. Suicide, yes – but I don't think it likely!

3. The Queen will abdicate, leaving Charles in command. This is the nicest interpretation of all the various aspects in force. After much heartbreak and worry, the Queen decides at the age of sixty-six that her 44-year-old son should take over the role as Head of State.

4. Something dramatic and perhaps violent will happen to the Royal Family itself and to the House of Windsor. Remember that the planet Pluto is not the only planet concerned. In the Queen's case, she has the three major outerspace planets locked in a firm embrace in her horoscope. Uranus and Neptune form a conjunction with her Ascendant. (They last formed a conjunction over a century ago, in the 1820s. The fact that it is taking place exactly on the Queen's Ascendant cannot be a coincidence.) At the same time, Pluto is conjunct her Midheaven and, in March 1993, Saturn conjunct her Mars.

It is perfectly credible that a revolution will sweep through Britain and obliterate the Royal Family. Certainly these heavenly forces are powerful enough to correspond with such an upheaval.

There is a fifth possibility. The Uranus–Neptune conjunction on the Queen's Ascendant can be seen simply in its negative interpretation as forces of rebellion and muddle. But there is a more sublime meaning, for Uranus symbolizes the occult power of the Age of Aquarius – the new Age of spiritual science towards which the world is speeding at this moment. Neptune, too, symbolizes the mystic power of the spirit. At their last conjunction, in the 1820s, Europe experienced the Romantic Movement – a welling-up of the spirit that found expression in poetry, paintings and novels which form the high-point of British culture to this day.

Perhaps, just perhaps, there will be an artistic and spiritual awakening in the 1990s to rival the glories of that previous age. Perhaps the ancient spiritual fires that burn in Britain will be kindled into bright flames. Perhaps they will be focused on the soul of Elizabeth and her family so that the House of Windsor will shine with inspiration that all the world can see.

Perhaps.

But I must warn Her Majesty, just as a final word, that the *next* previous Uranus–Neptune conjunction, before the 1820s one, was back in the seventeenth century. In the middle, actually. Well, to be absolutely honest, it was exact in – er, 1649, the year that Charles I was beheaded.

Ah well, let's not be superstitious.

			Sun	Moon	Mercury	Venus	Mars	Jupiter	Saturn	Uranus	Neptune	Pluto
	Asc	Mid	☉	☽	☿	♀	♂	♃	♄	♅	♆	♇
Victoria	6♊	2♒	2♊	4♊	9♉	27♈	18♈	17♒	29♓	23♐	29♐	27♓
Albert	12♍	6♊	2♍	2♏	22♍	20♌	23♊	10♒	29♓	21♐	26♐	27♓
Edward VII	28♐	3♏	16♏	29♍	0♐	19♎	15♑	21♐	0♑	21♓	14♒	19♈
Alexandra	?	?	9♐	19♌	17♐	0♏	28♎	24♓	3♒	2♈	21♒	22♈
Eddie	10♍	4♊	18♑	12♑	7♒	3♐	16♐	22♏	18♎	22♊	3♈	10♉
George V	2♈	1♑	12♊	1♎	18♉	10♉	5♌	25♐	24♎	28♊	10♈	13♉
Mary	6♒	6♐	5♊	8♓	29♉	3♉	15♌	6♓	19♏	6♋	14♈	11♉
Edward VIII	3♒	4♐	2♋	3♓	27♋	23♉	0♈	18♊	18♎	11♏	13♊	10♊
Wallis	25♋	9♈	28♊	12♎	16♉	23♊	21♈	8♌	12♏	21♏	18♊	12♊
George VI	27♎	7♌	21♐	24♏	18♐	5♏	1♐	8♌	14♏	22♏	16♊	11♊
Queen Mother	21♎	29♋	11♌	20♏	6♌	8♌	26♊	1♐	29♐	8♐	28♊	17♊
Elizabeth II	21♑	25♏	0♉	12♌	4♈	13♓	20♒	22♒	24♏	27♓	22♌	12♋
Philip	?♐	?	19♊	22♌	13♋	5♉	24♊	10♍	18♍	9♓	11♌	7♋
Charles	5♌	13♈	22♏	0♉	6♏	16♎	20♐	29♐	5♍	29♊	14♎	16♌
Anne	25	3♌	22♌	14♍	18♍	28♋	2♏	3♓	18♍	7♋	15♎	17♌
Mark	6♌♎	15♈	28♍	9♉	24♎	14♌	12♏	21♐	0♍	0♋	12♎	15♌

Andrew	11♌	23♈	0♓	25♏	17♓	28♑	27♑	28♐	14♑	18♌	9♏	5♍
Edward	16♎	22♋	20♓	9♒	17♓	3♉	15♓	22♈	28♒	7♍	17♏	12♍
Margaret	6♈	2♑	28♌	23♋	24♍	12♎	12♋	12♋	5♑	15♈	3♍	20♒
Tony	2♓	19♐	15♓	4♊	25♒	22♓	8♊	8♊	10♑	9♈	1♍	17♒
Lord Lindley	22♐	26♎	10♍	14♍	22♎	20♎	22♏	29♑	24♑	0♍	11♏	9♍
Lady Sarah	2♋	26♒	10♉	1♑	4♉	24♊	25♈	4♉	3♓	6♍	16♏	11♍
Duke of Gloucester	27♎	6♌	3♍	26♏	22♍	19♍	28♍	6♍	8♋	13♊	2♎	9♌
Duchess of Gloucester	?	?	28♊	?♓	19♋	2♌	0♍	17♎	24♋	18♊	5♎	9♌
Earl of Ulster	13♌	25♈	0♏	10♒	3♏	26♎	27♎	8♓	18♒	28♎	7♐	7♎
Duke of Kent	0♍	20♌	14♎	1♓	2♏	8♍	15♐	23♏	4♉	4♉	15♍	27♒
Duchess of Kent	?	?	3♓	?	15♓	18♒	13♍	20♍	10♒	20♈	8♒	21♋
Earl of St Andrews	24♎	3♌	4♋	26♈	14♊	11♌	21♉	12♓	10♒	27♌	11♏	8♍
Lady Helen Windsor	3♐	29♍	8♉	2♐	6♉	22♊	23♈	4♉	3♓	6♍	16♏	11♍
Lord Nicholas Windsor	7♑	12♏	2♌	8♉	2♌	15♍	4♌	27♎	21♉	5♎	28♏	25♍
Prince Michael	?	?	11♋	?	20♊	7♊	12♌	5♋	7♊	2♊	27♍	4♌
Princess Alexandra	15♓	24♐	3♑	26♉	22♑	16♒	23♎	5♑	16♓	5♉	18♍	28♋
Angus Ogilvy	0♍	17♉	21♍	22♍	12♎	11♎	21♊	10♉	13♐	5♈	29♌	18♋
James Ogilvy	14♋	12♓	10♓	3♎	28♒	22♈	7♓	20♈	27♒	8♍	17♏	13♍
Marina Ogilvy	22♑	26♏	8♌	1♒	2♌	12♋	14♋	19♋	20♓	17♍	19♏	16♍